CLOSER TO THE SELF

A FRAMEWORK FOR A RESTLESS WORLD

NANDI

Copyright Page

Closer to the Self

ISBN: 979-8-9957861-0-8

First edition, 2026

Printed in the United States of America

For permissions, inquiries, and future releases, please contact:
hello@satjana.com

Published by Satjana Editorial

CONTENTS

ABOUT THE AUTHOR

About Nandi

Nandi writes not as a teacher, but as a fellow traveler. Someone who studies, practices, and reflects on the timeless guidance of the sages through the lens of modern life.

I chose the name Nandi because, in the old stories, it points to joyful stillness and quiet strength. It points to the part of us that can wait patiently until clarity returns. The name also keeps attention off the person behind the words, so the focus stays on the inquiry itself. Behind it is an ordinary human being who has moved through confusion, restlessness, and searching, and found in the sages' framework a steady light.

A note on "the sages"

When this book says "the sages," it is not pointing to a vague idea or a myth. It points to real men and women across time who explored the mind and consciousness with unusual depth. Some lived as householders, some as renunciants, some as teachers, and many quietly unknown. What they shared was not theory first, but lived seeing. They tested attention, desire, and identity directly, and spoke from experience of greater clarity and inner alignment.

A note on change

This book is not asking you to become a different person overnight. It is offering small ways to see and test things as you read. If something here is real, it will show up in ordinary moments. A little more space before we react. A little less need to prove. A little more steadiness when life gets loud.

The sages called this inner treasure *daivi sampat*, but we can say it simply. Growth looks like fewer inner storms and more quiet strength. Not because we learned more words, but because the heart and mind began to move with more clarity and care.

Over time I learned something simple. When we understand how awareness, energy, and thought move within us, life becomes easier to navigate. Not because everything becomes perfect, but because we begin to see more clearly. What is shared here comes from that lived process. Not to instruct, but to make clarity feel gentle, practical, and grounded in everyday life.

Each idea in these pages invites reflection, not belief. Nothing is imposed. Everything is an invitation to test in the laboratory of your own daily life. The truth of these pointers is not in the words, but in the direct experience they unlock for you. There is no ideology to join and no identity to adopt. Only an encouragement to look directly, think clearly, and live consciously.

The language of Closer to the Self is deliberately plain, because wisdom is not hidden in complexity. It is revealed through clarity. These reflections are not meant to impress. They are meant to awaken your own seeing.

Nandi remains a student, observing, refining, and learning every day. This book is an offering of that ongoing practice. To understand the mind, to live with awareness, and to contribute, however quietly, to reducing confusion and kindling light in the human journey.

INTRODUCTION

Life as It Is Today

We live in a world full of movement, yet something in us longs for stillness. We have more connection, more stimulation, and more convenience than any generation before us. Yet beneath all the activity, many of us feel a quiet dissatisfaction we cannot name.

We get inspired and decide to change. A new routine, a diet, or a productivity method gives us hope. For a brief time, we feel stronger, clearer, and more focused.

But the spark fades. Old habits return, enthusiasm weakens, and we slip back into familiar patterns. This cycle repeats so often that we begin to treat it as normal, as if life is meant to be lived in short bursts of effort followed by collapse.

Deep down, we sense this cannot be the whole story. There must be a steadier way to live with clarity and joy, a way that does not depend on temporary motivation, but on something more stable within us.

The Cycles We Get Trapped In

If we look closely, many of us live in repeating cycles. We feel restless with the way things are, so we reach for something new. A fresh routine, a new app, a challenge, or a plan brings a burst of energy. For a while, it feels as if life is finally shifting.

But slowly the momentum fades. The routine slips, the habits return, and what felt like a breakthrough begins to feel like another effort that could not last. We promise ourselves we will try again, yet the same pattern quietly repeats.

This does not mean we lack sincerity or strength. It shows that our efforts are resting on ground that is not steady. We try to rebuild our lives without a foundation strong enough to hold what we create.

It is like placing stones on soft sand. No matter how carefully they are arranged, they cannot hold for long.

Lasting change needs something deeper to support it. Without that inner stability, even our most inspired efforts lose strength over time. The real question is not how to force change, but how to stand on firmer ground.

Why We Need a Framework

The problem is rarely a lack of effort. Most of us try sincerely. We set goals, make plans, and push ourselves toward change. But effort alone is fragile when it rests on shifting moods and circumstances. Some days we feel strong. Other days the same determination fades without warning.

Small goals can inspire us, yet they do not hold us steady for long. Health, success, recognition, and stability all matter, but they cannot anchor us by themselves. When our motivation depends on how we feel on a particular day, it rises and falls with the mind.

What we truly need is not another method, but a framework. Something that steadies us when enthusiasm fades and reminds us why we began. A framework keeps us aligned even when life becomes unpredictable. It provides a direction that does not change with every emotion or challenge.

When the framework points toward something deeper, the rest of life begins to settle naturally. Actions become more consistent. Choices become clearer. And the cycle of starting and stopping begins to ease, because we are no longer relying on motivation alone. We are standing on something more stable.

The Higher Aim

Imagine trying to balance one stone on top of another. A small shift or a single gust of wind can topple the effort, and everything must be rebuilt again. But if you begin by laying a strong foundation, stability becomes part of the structure itself.

Life works in much the same way. When we aim only for limited goals, we may achieve them for a time, but the results rarely last. The victories feel temporary because the ground beneath them keeps shifting. We find ourselves chasing improvement without feeling truly anchored.

When we aim for the highest goal, the discovery of the Self, everything else begins to align more naturally. Health, joy, clarity, and steadiness do not need to be forced in the same way. They begin to arise from a deeper source.

Instead of trying to manage each part of life separately, we nourish the deeper source from which all parts of life grow.

When that source becomes steadier, thought, action, and feeling begin to fall into better alignment.

What This Book Offers

This book is an invitation to explore such a framework. It is not a passing method or a burst of motivation, but a way of seeing shaped through centuries of human reflection. It is offered as a perspective, not as a rule to follow.

We may approach it through different doorways. Reflection, devotion, inquiry, stillness, or service can all lead toward the **same** understanding, because the principles beneath them are universal.

This framework was never meant only for monks or scholars. It was lived in villages and cities, by people raising families, working, creating, and searching for meaning in the midst of ordinary life.

It does not ask us to escape the world. It asks us to look at it with clearer eyes. Understanding this framework is not a weekend project. It is a lifelong journey. Yet even a small shift in how we see can change how each day feels.

Work becomes lighter. Relationships soften. The same routine becomes a field of growth rather than strain. This book is offered in that spirit.

Each chapter opens another layer of the journey. Each story holds a reminder. Each reflection serves as a mirror, helping us see the restlessness we all share with a little more clarity.

The Mind: Bondage or Release

At the center of all human experience is the mind. Many traditions have said the mind can either bind us or free us, and this remains true today. Everything depends on how it is understood and guided.

The mind is not the enemy. It is the instrument through which clarity or confusion appears.

When left untended, the mind drifts into cycles of habit, fear, and distraction. This is especially true in modern life, where constant notifications and endless stimulation amplify inner restlessness. Thoughts pull us in many directions at once, scattering attention and draining energy.

But when the mind is understood, it becomes a bridge between confusion and clarity. It can carry us toward steadiness with the same power it once used to create turmoil.

The mind cannot be subdued through force. It behaves like fog. No amount of pushing can make it disappear. A strong effort may clear it for a moment, but soon the mist returns. The more we resist it, the denser it becomes.

To work with the mind, we need a subtler approach, one that meets it with respect rather than struggle. We can begin by working with the mind through three complementary ways.

Story and metaphor help the mind feel what reason alone cannot always hold.

Observation helps us notice patterns gently, seeing how thoughts arise, fade, and return, and how tendencies repeat until they are understood.

Structure gives steadiness to what insight begins to reveal, creating simple rhythms that gradually turn restlessness into flow.

With artistry, observation, and structure together, the fog of the mind begins to thin. The same mind that once scattered our attention becomes a lens through which awareness shines. As clarity deepens, what once pulled us down begins to lift us up.

The Pull Toward the Self

If we observe our lives closely, the moments when we feel most alive are rarely the ones where we gain something. They are the moments when we feel more ourselves. A quiet walk, a heartfelt conversation, an act of kindness, or even a brief pause of stillness touches something deeper than circumstance.

There is a gentle pull at the center of these moments. The closer we come to this inner place, the more fulfilled and grounded we feel. Life does not become narrower when we move inward. It becomes fuller. Colors seem brighter, burdens grow lighter, and ordinary tasks carry a quiet radiance.

Whether we realize it or not, we are already moving toward this closeness. Some search for it through achievement. Others through relationships, learning, creativity, reflection, or service. Each of us follows a different path, yet we are all drawn by the same wish, to feel whole.

But longing by itself is not enough. Without direction, it appears only in brief flashes and then fades. We need a path that helps this closeness become steadier and more lived, so this sense of fullness does not remain a rare moment of luck.

In these quiet moments of clarity, a natural question arises.

Who am I, really, beneath all the roles and identities I have taken on?

Choosing a Framework

This book follows a path shaped by the wisdom of the sages, a way of seeing refined through centuries of reflection on the mind, the Self, and the deeper truth of life.

Over time, these teachings became a clear way of understanding life. They still speak to us today.

This path was not meant only for monks or scholars. It was also lived by ordinary people, people with families, work, responsibilities, and daily struggles. Its ideas are practical. Its examples are simple. Its guidance can be used in everyday life.

That is why this book begins here. It begins with the understanding that true fulfillment comes from coming closer to the Self. The sages offered a steady path for that journey.

This book does not ask us to leave life behind. It invites us to understand life more deeply and to live with greater clarity.

This book is not a lecture. It is a companion for the journey. It uses stories, reflections, and simple reasoning to help us move through confusion and come closer to clarity.

A Gentle Invitation

Some parts of this book may feel familiar at once, as if they are naming something already half known. Other parts may take longer to become clear. Not every idea opens in the same moment.

At times, a story, a metaphor, or a question may stay in the mind and return later in a quiet way. It may remain in the background of the day without asking for an immediate answer. This too is part of understanding.

Clarity does not always arrive through effort. Often it appears gradually, the way fog thins when light begins to grow.

This book is offered in that spirit. Not as something to push through, but as something that may stay near and become clearer in its own time.

How to Use This Framework

This book offers pointers from the sages, signposts that can help steady the inner landscape. They are not rigid instructions. They are suggestions shaped by centuries of human reflection, meant to be held lightly and tested in daily life.

Each of us carries a different mind and nervous system, shaped by circumstances, tendencies, and needs. For that reason, no single formula serves everyone in the same way. Understanding grows at its own rhythm, and the insights that matter most are the ones that feel alive and useful in ordinary moments.

The emphasis here is not on scholarly detail or technical concepts. It is on clarity in plain language, so the ideas can be lived rather than memorized. These reflections are meant to be practical. They can fit into the flow of a normal day, opening small spaces of awareness where ease can enter.

If these chapters help you feel even a little closer to the Self, and if the metaphors become part of your own way of seeing, then the purpose of this book is fulfilled.

Clarity begins the moment we turn inward. We begin with what most of us recognize immediately, the fog that covers the inner sky even when life looks fine from the outside.

PART ONE
THE HUMAN CONDITION

CHAPTER 1

THE FOG OF CONFUSION

IGNORANCE AS THE VEIL OF CLARITY

The Fog

There are mornings when fog covers everything. The road is still there, the trees are still there, the houses are still there, yet we cannot see them clearly. The world has not vanished, but our vision of it is blurred.

This is how many of us live. We have families, work, opportunities, and yet something remains hidden. Life itself is present, but we cannot see it clearly. Sometimes the fog is made of pain, old hurts, disappointments, or unfinished stories from the past. We are not broken. The light has only been covered for a while.

The sages gave a name to this condition: ignorance of our true Self. Ignorance here does not mean a lack of information. We may have libraries of facts in our heads and still miss the essence. It means forgetting what we are at the deepest level, mistaking the fog for reality, and forgetting the sky behind it. Holding a clear crystal under dim light, it appears dark. The light is not absent. It simply does not pass through fully. It is like the sun hidden by thick clouds. Its brilliance remains, though the sight of it is lost.

Not All Fog Is Everywhere

It is important to see clearly. The fog does not cover everything. Each of us carries some area of life where clarity already shines. For some, it is in work, a natural discipline, a talent, or a gift honed over time. For others, it is in relationships, the ability to listen, to love, to forgive. For still others, it may be creativity, service, or devotion.

The sages never said we are hopelessly bound. They said we are already partly free. The fog may blur certain parts of our vision, but in other areas the path is steady and bright. These are not accidents. They are often the results of past effort and grace.

Our journey is not to build clarity from scratch, but to extend the clarity we already have into the places where fog still lingers. Like a lamp in a dark room, even a small light gradually spreads. It often helps to begin with what already feels natural and steady within you.

When discipline comes naturally, it can steady reflection. When compassion flows easily, it can soften what anger has hardened. When reasoning is sharp, it can question old assumptions.

In this way, our strengths become ropes tied to solid ground, helping us cross the foggy patches. From what is clear, we move toward what is clouded. From what shines in us, we let the light spread into darker corners. The fog is real, but it is never complete. Something in us always remembers the light, even when it feels far away. That quiet remembering keeps despair from taking root and opens the door to hope.

. . .

The light within us is real, but when the fog thickens, even that light can seem to waver. Understanding how this happens helps us stay patient with ourselves and others.

The Short-Circuiting of Energies

When fog thickens in the mind, even our noblest qualities become distorted. The current of energy that should flow clearly gets diverted and expressed in a lower form.

- Love becomes possessiveness
- Compassion hardens into cruelty
- Courage turns into aggression
- Confidence inflates into arrogance
- Desire becomes craving
- Greed steals contentment
- Delusion clouds clarity

These are not our true nature. These are energies that become short circuited by confusion. The very force that turns into jealousy is born of love. The pride that blinds us is rooted in healthy confidence. When the fog lifts, these energies return to their original form, love, compassion, courage, confidence, shining naturally as part of who we are.

Think of electricity. When it flows through the proper channel, it lights the lamp. If the wire is broken or misdirected, sparks fly, heat builds, and damage occurs. The energy itself is not bad. It is simply misplaced. So it is with us.

Ignorance is not a permanent stain. It does not add anything foreign to us. It only misdirects what is already ours. It is like clear water appearing muddy when stirred. The water itself has not changed. When still, the clarity returns. This is why the sages insist: you are not broken, only covered.

. . .

The Third Eye and Horizontal Vision

Most of us live with a horizontal vision of time. Our eyes and our thoughts are fixed on the line that stretches between past and future. We replay yesterday's mistakes, we anticipate tomorrow's outcomes, and so we miss the only reality that exists: the present moment.

The sages use the third eye as an allegory. The two horizontal eyes are bound to the line of past and future. But when the third eye opens, we are pulled into the vertical axis of the present.

To live with the third eye open is not a mystical feat. It simply means to be fully here, in this breath, this step, this conversation. When the fog of memory and projection clears, the present moment reveals itself as fresh, unburdened, alive.

Think of a film reel. Each frame exists only for an instant, but when strung together, it creates the illusion of a flowing story. In the same way, the mind stitches together fragments of past and future, weaving them into what feels like reality. But the only frame that is ever real is the one showing right now.

Another parable says there are two birds sitting on the same tree. One eats sweet and bitter fruits. The other simply watches in silence. We live as the bird that eats, tasting pleasure and pain, pulled into past and future. But our deeper Self is the silent bird, ever present, watching without being caught. Recognizing the silent bird within, even for a moment, is to glimpse the third eye opening.

Ignorance is what makes us forget the present. We wander into shadows of memory or projections of possibility, and so the real slips through unnoticed. Knowledge, then, is not about piling up more information about the past or speculating about the future. It is about recognition, seeing the Self here and now. When we return to this moment, the fog begins to lift, and with it comes a quiet freedom: the ability to live, not just to remember or to anticipate.

Seeing clearly is one part of the journey. But clarity does not last when the mind is restless. So the sages also point to steadiness, a mind calm enough to reflect truth without distortion.

The Dusty Mirror

The sages often compared the mind to a mirror. A clean mirror reflects reality as it is. But when covered with dust, it shows distorted or dim images. So it is with us. The Self always shines, but the dust of ignorance, desires, fears, comparisons, restlessness, prevents a clear reflection.

When we polish the mirror, we do not create new light. We simply allow what is already shining to be seen. In daily life, polishing the mirror means quieting restlessness, reducing unnecessary desires, and returning to simplicity. It is an inner movement, not an outer rearrangement, a gentle turning of attention toward what is already clear within. The process is gradual, but every small act of awareness clears away a little more dust. Yet when the mirror remains dusty, attention naturally turns outward, seeking brightness elsewhere.

The Search Outside

When the fog hides our own light, the mind naturally turns outward. It runs toward things to see, hear, taste, touch, and hold. This outward movement of thought is not a flaw. It is simply how the mind works. Its currents flow outward through the senses, chasing objects and experiences.

At first this seems harmless, even promising. Perhaps peace will be found in possessions, in achievements, in recognition. But each success is temporary. The moment one desire is met, another rises, and the mind rushes after it like a river always seeking the sea.

A parable tells of a woman who lost her necklace and searched frantically everywhere, in cupboards, in corners, even in the streets. At last, a friend pointed to her own neck. The necklace had been there all along. So it is with us. We search everywhere for happiness, forgetting that the treasure rests quietly within. The mind, flowing outward, misses what is nearest.

The sages point out that the same currents of thought that flow outward can be gently turned inward. Instead of endlessly reaching for the next image, object, or achievement, the mind can learn to rest in its own source. This is not suppression but redirection, like a river flowing back toward its spring.

Ignorance makes us believe that peace lies somewhere else. We chase reflections, mistaking their glimmer for substance. There is nothing wrong with work, success, or beauty. Only the forgetting that their joy arises from within. When the current turns inward, we begin to see that what we sought outside was quietly shining within us all along.

What the Sages Point To

The sages offer a simple affirmation after we have already lived through this fog. The confusion we feel is not permanent. Anxiety is not our essence. Beneath the fog, our true nature is serene, whole, and untouched.

Ignorance covers but does not destroy. Just as fog hides the sun without ever extinguishing it, ignorance hides the Self without ever touching it.

. . .

One of the oldest parables says: in twilight, a rope on the ground is mistaken for a snake. Fear arises, the heart races, the body trembles. But when light is brought, the snake is gone. It was only ever a rope.

Our fears are real in their effect, but false in their foundation. They arise from a simple error, confusing what changes for what we truly are. This teaching does not create anything new. It simply shines the light that reveals what has always been present.

The Modern Restlessness

If ignorance was a fog in the past, in today's world it can feel like a storm. Phones buzz before one thought is complete. Screens flicker with endless images. We scroll through hundreds of faces but struggle to sit quietly with our own. The mind leaps like a monkey from one branch to another, restless and unsatisfied.

We mistake motion for progress, stimulation for joy. But in truth, this is restlessness. We are more connected yet feel more alone, more informed yet feel less certain, more active yet less at peace. These teachings remain timeless because they address the root, not the symptoms. They say we do not need more to become whole. We need to see more clearly.

Hope Beyond the Fog

The sages never condemned the fog. They did not ask why we are blind. They simply said, this is where you are, begin here. Ignorance is not an enemy to be destroyed. It is a condition to be understood. The moment we recognize it, clarity becomes possible.

Peace is not something we must manufacture. It is the quiet fragrance of the Self waiting to be uncovered. Realization does not create something new. It reveals what has always been true, like waking from a dream. One moment of clarity can dissolve years of confusion.

A Quiet Pause

When the mind grows noisy, the world grows small.
The future presses in, the past pulls tight,
and the present becomes a thin thread we can barely hold.

But beneath the fog there is always a faint glow.
A softness that does not argue.
A light that does not push.

It waits, like dawn behind the hills,
like a necklace already around the neck
that we keep searching for in every corner of the room.

Sometimes it appears for a breath
in a quiet morning
or in the pause after an emotion breaks open.

In that brief clarity,
the heart remembers something older than fear
and gentler than thought.

It remembers itself.

Let that memory rise for a moment.
Not fully, just as a feeling,
like a hand resting softly on your shoulder from behind.

The fog does not vanish at once.
But even a small opening
is enough for the light to begin its work.

. . .

Reflection for the Reader

Pause for a quiet moment and look gently at your own life. Notice if there is a place where the inner view feels blurred today, a worry about the future, a regret from the past, or a subtle comparison that steals your peace.

Instead of pushing it away or judging yourself, simply recognize the fog. Ask yourself what part of your inner landscape feels overshadowed right now.

See if you can sense how your energies shift.

Did love tighten into fear?
Did courage bend into impatience?
Did clarity slip into confusion without you noticing?

These changes happen quietly. Noticing them is the beginning of wisdom.

Now look at the direction of your attention.

Has it been reaching outward all day, searching for completion in tasks, people, outcomes, or distractions?

And what would it feel like, even for a breath, to pause, turn inward, and rest in the one place the fog cannot reach?

As you sit with these questions, you may sense a light beneath the haze, soft, steady, familiar. It has always been there. It is closer than you think.

Closing

The sages remind us that the fog is not final. It is a covering, not our essence. Beneath it, the Self remains whole, radiant, and untouched. As we come closer to that Self, serenity arises naturally. From that serenity, every part of life begins to shift, not through changing everything outside, but by opening a wider space of consciousness within what already is.

When the fog begins to lift within, it quietly reshapes how we move through the world.

If you are a mother, you may find yourself more patient and more tender. If you are a father, you may bring steadiness and warmth to your children. If you are a partner, you may listen more deeply. If you are a spiritual seeker, you may notice your questions soften and your journey feel more grounded and real. If you are a worker, an artist, a leader, or a student, your work may gain a quiet clarity. It becomes infused with presence, attention, and care.

Life does not need to be abandoned. It becomes more meaningful. The same actions, when rooted in serenity, carry a different fragrance. The ordinary becomes sacred. The repetitive becomes purposeful. Relationships become reflections of the peace touched within.

This is the promise the sages point to: not escape from life, but fullness in life. A rising tide does not replace the boats. It lifts them all. When consciousness clears and the Self is glimpsed, every aspect of life is lifted with it.

This book is about those ropes the sages left behind, frameworks to hold and stories to reflect upon, so we may clear the fog and see what has always been shining within. The fog is not a personal failure. It is part of the human journey.

Next, we look at the instrument through which the fog appears: the mind itself.

CHAPTER 2

THE MIRROR WITHIN

THE NATURE OF THE MIND AND ITS INSTRUMENTS

The Mirror and the Orchestra

In the first chapter we walked through the fog that hides the Self. Now we look at what creates that fog, the mind. The sages said the mind is a mirror. When clean, it reflects the serenity of the Self. When covered, it reflects confusion instead.

But that mirror is not made of a single piece of glass. It is an orchestra of subtle instruments, each with its role. When they play in tune, the reflection is bright. When they fall out of rhythm, the music becomes noise and fog fills the hall. This is where every human story begins, inside the orchestra pit of our own awareness.

The Flow of a Moment

You are walking home after a long day. Someone passes and mutters a rude comment. In an instant, the inner orchestra begins to play. This orchestra is not one voice. It is a few voices working together. When they play together, we stay clear. When they clash, the fog returns.

- **Manas** - the gatherer, catches the sound: "He insulted me."

• **Ahamkara** - the ego, leaps forward: "How dare he!"
• **Chitta** - the storehouse of memory, opens its old archives: "They always treat me this way."
• **Buddhi** - the quiet intellect, tries to speak: "Perhaps he's troubled. Let it go."

The sages said the mind is not one voice, but these parts working together. When they move together, we stay clear. When they pull apart, the fog returns. But the ego's drums are louder. You replay the words again and again, defending, explaining, judging. The more you think, the thicker the fog inside. Hours later, when the storm subsides, Buddhi's voice returns like a small breeze through smoke. The same incident now feels trivial. Nothing changed outside. Only clarity returned inside.

This is how the fog forms, and how it clears. Every moment of life moves through the same sequence:

perception → reaction → memory → reflection → peace

When these inner instruments play in harmony, the moment ends in understanding. When they clash, it ends in unrest. The sages said the mind is not one thing. It is this orchestra of four functions working together. When they move in tune, life feels clear. When they collide, fog returns.

The Four Functions Seen Clearly

Manas, The Messenger

When Manas is restless, it runs between ten thousand windows, reporting too much too fast. When calm, it delivers each impression gently, giving Buddhi space to see clearly.

. . .

Parable: The Messenger Who Wouldn't Pause

A king once appointed a swift messenger to carry news across his land. The man took pride in his speed. He galloped from village to village without stopping, shouting half the message at one place and mixing the rest with his own ideas at another. When he returned, the kingdom was in chaos. Soldiers moved where there was no war. Merchants closed their shops expecting invasion. Farmers fled their fields. The king sighed and said, "Had you rested between words, my kingdom would have rested too."

So it is with Manas. When it rushes from one impression to the next without pause, truth is lost in the noise. Rest, even for a breath, and clarity returns.

Buddhi, The Light of Discernment

Buddhi evaluates and guides. It asks, "Is this true? Is this useful? Is this kind?" It does not shout. It shines. When Buddhi leads, fog dissolves quickly. It knows that every emotion has meaning, but not every emotion deserves command. A lantern does not fight the darkness. It simply glows. Likewise, Buddhi clears confusion by seeing, not by struggling.

Ahamkara, The Claimant

Ahamkara gives individuality, the sense of I. Used rightly, it organizes life. "I will work. I will care for my family." But when it forgets its role, it tries to run the whole show.

It says, "I am the thinker, the doer, the enjoyer." Then every passing thought becomes personal. Anger becomes my anger. Sorrow becomes my wound. Ahamkara paints the fog with color, pride, jealousy, comparison. These turn passing clouds into storms of identity.

. . .

When Buddhi whispers, "That is enough," ego replies, "But I deserve more." When intellect advises restraint, ego paints pictures of deprivation. Ego's cleverness is that it uses even wisdom to serve itself.

Chitta, The Storehouse

Chitta is memory, not just recall, but the soil of tendencies. Every action, desire, and unspoken thought leaves a faint seed here. Most of the time those seeds sleep. But when Manas stirs them and ego waters them with attention, they sprout as habits and fears.

Parable: The Garden of the Mind

A gardener tended a small patch of land behind his home. Some days he planted flowers. Some days he tossed scraps and peels without thought. Months passed. Where he had planted roses, fragrance spread. Where he had thrown waste, weeds grew thick. Looking at the mixed garden, he sighed, "Every handful I threw has grown into something."

The mind is that garden. Every thought is a seed. Sow peace and you reap calm. Sow anger and you reap unrest. The sages said:

Sow a seed, and you reap a thought.
Sow a thought, and you reap an action.
Sow an action, and you reap a habit.
Sow a habit, and you reap a character.
Sow a character, and you reap a destiny.

Nothing in the mind truly disappears. It waits to sprout again. But the same law that binds also frees. Tend the garden with awareness, and the weeds of confusion slowly give way to flowers of clarity.

Chitta can be friend or foe. When purified through reflection and mindfulness, it becomes a garden of insight. When left unattended, it becomes the fog's reservoir, thick with old impressions.

How the Fog Forms Inside

The outer fog hides the world. The inner fog hides ourselves. It begins when the ego forgets its place. It takes what Buddhi concludes and twists it to its liking. It draws energy from memory, paints it with emotion, and floods the mind with restlessness.

Soon the messenger, Manas, brings distorted news. The advisor, Buddhi, is ignored. The king, Ego, grows loud. The record keeper, Chitta, keeps replaying the same story. That is the moment when the mirror loses its clarity. But an orchestra cannot stay in rhythm without a conductor. That silent conductor is Prana.

The Role of Prana, The Current Beneath the Mind

Behind every thought, emotion, and movement flows an invisible current of life, Prana. Prana is to the mind what electricity is to a lamp, unseen, but the source of all brightness.

It is the subtle energy that animates the body and carries the mind. Without it, the senses cannot perceive, the brain cannot think, and even the intellect remains still. The body is like a lamp, the mind like a filament, but Prana is the electricity that makes them glow.

. . .

We notice its presence whenever it changes. When Prana flows evenly, there is quiet alertness. Breathing feels easy. Thoughts move smoothly. Emotions stay light. When Prana is disturbed, everything ripples. The same event that felt simple a moment ago now feels unbearable. A little fatigue, a shallow breath, an unspoken worry, and the orchestra goes out of tune. It is not the world that changed. It is the current beneath it.

Prana is not breath, yet breath is its doorway. Each inhalation gathers energy. Each exhalation releases what is stagnant. The sages discovered that by steadying the rhythm of the breath, we can steady the rhythm of thought. When breath slows, Manas slows. When Manas slows, Buddhi begins to speak again. That is why every spiritual tradition, East or West, begins with a moment of conscious breathing before prayer or meditation. To calm the breath is to remind the orchestra of its natural rhythm.

There are many streams of this current. Some lift energy upward into inspiration and clarity. Some ground it downward into stability. Some distribute it evenly like the pulse of life through every limb. When these flows are balanced, the mind and body act as one instrument. When they are tangled, the fog thickens and the sense of harmony fades.

Modern life scatters Prana constantly, through overstimulation, hurried meals, irregular sleep, and constant mental strain. We keep our engines running while forgetting the fuel itself. Reconnecting with Prana does not require technique first. It requires remembrance. A slow walk in silence, a few deep breaths before speaking, a moment of gratitude before eating, these are simple ways of honoring the current that keeps us alive.

Prana is the bridge between the visible and the invisible. It links the physical body to the subtle mind and carries the light of awareness into action. When this current flows freely, Buddhi's clarity can reach every corner of our being, and life begins to move with quiet grace.

The sages called it the breath of the Self, not because the Self breathes, but because through this movement the stillness of the Self animates the world. When we attend to this current with care, we discover that peace is not a state we create. It is the natural rhythm of energy in harmony.

The Fog Begins to Clear

When Buddhi reawakens and Manas learns to pause, when ego softens and memory releases its grip, a remarkable thing happens. The same world looks different. Nothing external has changed, yet the air inside feels lighter.

The fog does not vanish all at once. It thins slowly, like morning mist lifting from a valley, letting glimpses of sunlight through. At first, we see only patches of blue between the clouds, but even those brief openings bring relief. Each moment of understanding is a small crack in the cloud through which light spills quietly back into life.

As stillness deepens, the mind begins to resemble a clear lake. When its surface is restless, it breaks the reflection of the sky into fragments. When it is still, the entire sky is mirrored in it without distortion. So too, when the mind is steady, it reflects the Self perfectly. The sky has always been there. The lake only needed to be calm enough to see it.

The same light that once seemed hidden now shines through every act and thought. We start to see people not as obstacles but as mirrors. Events not as interruptions but as part of a larger design. The fog becomes thin enough for the heart to recognize its own radiance again.

These moments of clarity come and go like sunlight through drifting clouds, but each one leaves behind a little more space inside. A space where peace can settle naturally. It is here that we begin to sense what the sages meant when they said, "The Self is ever revealed, but the mind must become still enough to notice."

A Quiet Pause

When the mind reacts, it can feel immediate,
as if there is no space
between the world
and our response.

Yet beneath that rush
there is always something quieter,
a simple noticing
before judgment,
a small pause
before we speak.

It is like sitting in a concert hall
before the orchestra begins.
Everything is still for a moment,
and we can feel
the quiet that was there all along.

Every reaction rises from that quiet
and returns to it,
the way sound fades
back into silence.

Sometimes we notice it by accident,
a pause before anger forms,
a softness before fear tightens,

a calm moment
inside the noise.

In those moments
the mind is not fighting itself.
It is remembering
there is a steady place inside
even while thoughts move.

Let attention rest there
for one breath.
Not as an idea,
but as a simple presence,
the space from which thoughts rise
and into which they return.

The mind does not need to be perfect
to reflect truth.
It only needs a moment of stillness
for the light to show through.

Reflection for the Reader

Pause for a moment and return to one experience from today, anything small, maybe a comment someone made, a message you received, or a moment that stirred emotion.

Hold it lightly, without judgment.

Now watch the orchestra within.
Notice how Manas rushes to bring the signal.
Notice how ego steps in quickly to claim it.
Notice how memory pulls old stories into the room without being invited.

Notice how Buddhi tries to speak, quietly, beneath the noise.

Which voice spoke the loudest in that moment?
Which one did you ignore?
Which one appeared too late?

These are not flaws. They are signals, the timing of the instruments that shape experience from the inside.

See if you can feel the exact moment when fog begins to form. A tightening in the chest. A sudden story in the mind. A quick impulse to react. And also see the moment when it begins to thin, a breath, a pause, a hint of understanding breaking through.

Let yourself observe all this with gentleness. This is not about stopping thoughts or silencing emotions. It is about recognizing the music your mind is already playing. If you listen carefully, you may hear a softer note beneath the noise, the quiet voice that waits for stillness to be heard. It is closer than you think.

Closing

The mind is the bridge between the Self and the world. When fog fills that bridge, everything feels heavy and confusing. When it clears, life flows with a quiet rhythm.

We do not destroy the ego or erase memory. We bring them into harmony with the light of Buddhi, the intellect. Then every thought, emotion, and action becomes transparent, not separate from the Self, but expressions of it.

The sages understood that clarity must be protected like a lamp in the wind. To help us keep the flame steady, they shaped gentle disciplines, yoga to align body and energy, pranayama to steady the life current, meditation to quiet the mind, mantra to refine vibration and focus awareness, self reflection to keep Buddhi awake, and devotion to soften the heart. Together they form a whole path, what later came to be called Integral Yoga, where thought, emotion, action, and energy all support one another.

These are not mechanical practices but creative tools, the art, science, and structure of inner life. Art gives sensitivity and beauty to the journey. Science brings observation and precision. Structure brings rhythm and steadiness. When these blend, practice becomes joyful, balanced, and sustainable. Through them, the fog does not return as heavily, because the light is being tended daily.

Later in this book we will explore these pathways more closely. How movement, breath, reflection, love, and service each open a different window toward clarity. They are the ropes the sages left behind for those of us walking through the mist, simple tools that remind us of what is already shining within.

These practices are not escapes from life but ways of deepening it. They keep the mirror polished even while life continues to move, reminding us again and again that peace is not elsewhere. It is the natural fragrance of a clear mind.

When we begin to understand the mind rather than fight it, every part of life starts to feel more spacious and clear. If you are a mother, you may notice your reactions soften as you understand the movements of your own mind. If you are a father, you may find steadiness growing as you see how thoughts rise and fall without needing to be followed. If you are a partner, you may listen more openly, sensing the difference between what is true and what is only a passing impulse. If you are a spiritual seeker, you may feel your journey deepen as you learn to watch the mind instead of being carried by it. If you are a worker, an artist, a leader, or a student, you may discover that clarity of mind brings clarity to every action, allowing you to move with focus, presence, and ease.

Nothing is lost. Everything becomes more luminous. This is the beginning of true clarity, not a new mind, but a clearer mirror.

In the next chapter we will explore what gives this mirror its color, the three gunas, the subtle forces of nature that tint every experience with lightness, passion, or inertia.

CHAPTER 3

THREADS OF THE SELF

THE PLAY OF THE THREE GUṆAS

The Threads of Nature

Why is the mind calm one day, restless the next, and heavy on another? Why do moods, thoughts, and energies shift without reason?

The sages offered a simple and profound key. Everything in nature, from the smallest atom to the largest star, from a single thought to the entire universe, is woven from three qualities, three strands called gunas. They are like threads in a single rope, always intertwined, never separate. These three are Sattva, Rajas, and Tamas.

Sattva is clarity and light.
Rajas is motion and desire.
Tamas is inertia and darkness.

All three together form the living fabric of experience. The balance among them determines how we feel, act, and perceive the world.

. . .

The Three Qualities

Sattva, Clarity and Light
Purity, harmony, joy, and wisdom. Sattva is like a calm lake reflecting the sky without distortion. It brings balance, contentment, and compassion. When Sattva predominates, the heart feels peaceful, the mind is alert but not restless, and life flows effortlessly. We feel at home within ourselves.

Rajas, Activity and Motion
Desire, ambition, restlessness, and passion. Rajas is like a whirlwind stirring dust into the air. It fuels creation, progress, and movement, but it also brings attachment, competition, and fatigue. When Rajas predominates, the mind is constantly reaching, planning, comparing, striving. There is excitement, but not peace.

Tamas, Inertia and Darkness
Laziness, confusion, heaviness, and ignorance. Tamas is like a thick fog that hides the path. It brings forgetfulness, resistance, and apathy. When Tamas predominates, we feel dull, indifferent, or trapped. The light of clarity seems far away, yet it is only hidden behind the clouds.

No person, object, or thought is free of these three. They are always present in shifting proportions, like colors blending on a painter's palette.

Parable: The Three Painters
Three painters were asked to depict the same sunrise. The Sattvic painter used soft, balanced tones that captured the serenity

of the morning. The Rajasic painter worked with great energy, his brush flying fast, his painting brilliant but restless. The Tamasic painter left the canvas half finished, the colors heavy and dull.

Each saw the same world, but painted through the color of his mind. So it is with us. We all experience the same life, but our perception is colored by whichever guna predominates within us.

The Dance of the Three Currents

The gunas never appear alone. They move together like three currents in the same river. At any moment, one may rise higher, another fall, but all three remain present in shifting proportions.

- Sattva gives clarity.
- Rajas gives movement.
- Tamas gives structure and rest.

In every thought, every emotion, every action, all three blend together like light, color, and shadow creating a single scene. When Sattva rises, the mind feels peaceful, not because Rajas and Tamas vanished, but because they have taken supportive roles. When Rajas surges, it does not destroy Sattva or Tamas. It simply drowns their voices for a while. And when Tamas grows heavy, it is not darkness alone. It carries within it the potential for stillness and renewal once the fog lifts.

Understanding this is crucial. The mind is not good on some days and bad on others. It is simply reflecting whichever guna is strongest in that moment. This allows compassion. This allows patience. This prevents self judgment. The inner weather changes, but the sky behind it remains the same.

To work with the gunas is not to fight them, but to see them clearly, and through that clarity, gently guide their proportions. This awareness is the beginning of mastery. With this understanding in place, we can watch how these currents rise and fall through an ordinary day.

The Sky We Live In

The gunas do not only shape mood. They shape the very space we think we live in.

When **Tamas** dominates, the world feels like a small room. Walls seem solid and close. Life shrinks to the body and the senses. The weather is thick. Awareness narrows. We feel confined inside our own thoughts. This is the space of contraction.

When **Rajas** dominates, the world becomes a rush of wind. Ideas, desires, and worries pull the mind in every direction. The weather is restless. Even in a still body, the mind is running. We live in motion, chasing meaning but unable to rest in it. This is the space of striving.

When **Sattva** dominates, the walls dissolve and the inner sky opens. Thoughts pass like light clouds. The weather is calm. There is room to breathe, room to feel, room to understand. We discover a quiet space inside that was always waiting. This is the space of clarity.

The sages say these are not fantasies of the mind. They are shifts in the inner space with which we identify. Tamas keeps us in the room. Rajas sweeps us into the wind. Sattva reveals the open sky.

And deeper than all weather is the space that never changes. A silent, endless sky that holds every moment of life without being touched by any of them. It does not appear when the mind is clear. It is already here, beneath fog, storm, and sunlight alike.

We do not climb to a higher place when peace rises. We simply stop falling into clouds. The sky is not found. It is remembered. The Self is the sky. The mind is the weather. The gunas are the shifting seasons. As clarity expands, we begin to live less in the weather and more in the sky.

How the Gunas Move Within Us

The three gunas are not fixed. They rise and fall in endless rhythm.

- When **Sattva** predominates, we feel light, joyful, and clear. The mind is quiet, and decisions come naturally. The world seems luminous. Even ordinary moments feel sacred.
- When **Rajas** predominates, the mind rushes outward. Desire, ambition, and restlessness drive every action. We work hard, but rarely feel satisfied.
- When **Tamas** predominates, energy sinks. We procrastinate, avoid effort, and confuse comfort with peace. The same world that once inspired us now feels dull and meaningless.

The gunas shift throughout the day. After rest, Sattva rises. During work, Rajas dominates. Late at night, Tamas returns. They shape not only mood but perception itself. A person full of Rajas may see opportunity in every event. The same event looks threatening to someone ruled by Tamas, and serene to one steeped in Sattva.

The mind is the stage. The gunas are the actors. Their changing proportions create the play of our inner world.

The Gunas at Work in a Modern Day

From dawn to nightfall, the three gunas dance through our lives. They shift quietly with food, company, thought, and circumstance, shaping how the mind feels and acts.

. . .

Morning: The Rise of Sattva

When the body wakes rested and the breath is calm, Sattva is already near. The mind, Manas, feels light, the intellect, Buddhi, clear. Reflection comes easily, perhaps a short prayer, a walk in silence, or simple gratitude for the new day. In this clarity, ego, Ahamkara, loosens. It does not rush to claim the morning. Memory, Chitta, feels clean, free from yesterday's noise.

Decisions made in this mood are wise and gentle. Sattva gives direction without strain. The orchestra plays in tune.

Midday: The Surge of Rajas

As work begins, Rajas steps forward. Energy rises, goals call, movement fills the hours. Rajas is necessary. It gives momentum and drive, but if unbalanced it overwhelms Buddhi's calm voice. Manas races between tasks. Ego starts claiming credit or fearing failure. Chitta digs out comparisons and old insecurities.

Soon, the same energy that fueled creativity becomes agitation. When Rajas dominates, the intellect becomes a servant to the ego. We still achieve, but joy fades.

Evening: The Pull of Tamas

After long activity, the pendulum swings. Fatigue, heaviness, and dullness settle in. The mind seeks escape rather than rest. Scrolling endlessly, overeating, or drifting into complaint are Tamas in disguise.

Here, Manas loses alertness, Buddhi withdraws, and ego clings to comfort. "I deserve this numbness." If allowed to rule, Tamas turns rest into inertia. But when met with awareness, a quiet meal, deep breathing, or reflection, Tamas transforms into true rest, preparing the way for Sattva to return at dawn.

. . .

Thus within one ordinary day, all three gunas complete their cycle. Sattva inspires, Rajas acts, Tamas restores. When balanced, they serve one another. When exaggerated, they obscure the Self. This same rhythm appears not only across a full day, but even in the smallest act.

Everyday Example: The Morning Walk

Consider something as ordinary as beginning a morning walk or fitness routine. The first few days feel fresh and joyful. The early air feels pure, the body light, the mind calm. There is quiet enthusiasm, a natural rhythm between breath and step.

This is Sattva, clarity, balance, and harmony at the beginning of effort. Soon, as progress shows, Rajas awakens. The mind begins to plan, to measure, to compare. "How many steps did I do yesterday? Can I go faster today?" Energy rises, but peace fades. The same walk that began as self care becomes a race. Rajas pushes forward, restless to achieve more, and the joy of the walk begins to turn into pressure.

Weeks later, fatigue creeps in. Tamas appears quietly. The alarm rings and the thought comes, "Maybe tomorrow." One missed day becomes several. The shoes gather dust. The same activity that once lifted energy now feels heavy. The mind justifies in whispers. "I'm tired. It doesn't matter." This is Tamas, heaviness, resistance, and withdrawal.

Then one morning, without any grand plan, you step out again. The air feels kind, the light soft. There's no goal this time, no measuring, only movement and breath. That simple act of returning, without pressure, without pride, is Sattva reborn.

The same path, the same body, but a clearer state of mind. This is how the gunas move within us. Clarity gives birth to effort. Effort turns into restlessness. Restlessness falls into dullness. Dullness gives way again to renewed clarity.

The cycle itself is not wrong. It is the natural breathing of energy through life. Awareness of this movement is what transforms it from compulsion into understanding. When we learn to see it clearly, we no longer swing blindly between extremes. We begin to walk with life, not against it.

Creating Through the Gunas

The gunas also shape our larger journeys, the way we build, create, and bring ideas into the world. Imagine an entrepreneur beginning a new company. At the start, there is inspiration, a clear vision to serve, to innovate, to create something meaningful. Ideas come effortlessly. The direction feels right. This is Sattva guiding from within, the light of clarity and purpose that points true north.

As plans turn into action, Rajas takes charge. Meetings, designs, deadlines, negotiations, motion fills every day. Rajas is the energy of creation itself. It gives courage, initiative, and drive. But when it grows unchecked, pressure replaces inspiration. The same fire that once illuminated now begins to burn. Impatience grows. Rest is forgotten. The mind starts living in outcomes rather than the joy of doing.

Then, after a long strain, Tamas quietly appears. The body tires. The mind doubts. Enthusiasm wanes. Thoughts like “I can’t do this” or “It’s too much” take root. Work feels heavy. Meaning fades. Nothing is wrong when this happens. It is simply nature calling for balance.

. . .

Yet with awareness, even this phase has purpose. Rest is not the end of effort, but its renewal. Stepping back, sleeping well, walking in nature, rest restores balance. Slowly, the inner light of Sattva returns. With clarity regained, effort becomes wiser. Rajas now works under guidance rather than impulse, and Tamas becomes the ground of stability rather than inertia.

Through this rhythm of clarity, action, and rest, ideas mature into reality. Every success, whether worldly or spiritual, is born through this dance of the gunas. This rhythm appears everywhere, building a company, writing a book, raising a child, deepening a meditation practice. Sattva gives direction. Rajas performs. Tamas anchors.

When they move in balance, creation flourishes. When one dominates, imbalance follows. The wise do not fight this rhythm. They learn to tune it. They pause when rest is needed, act when clarity calls, and reflect when noise grows too loud.

It is not by suppressing any guna, but by recalibrating their proportions, that great works take shape. In this way, even the building of a company becomes a spiritual act, an expression of the same universal law that moves the stars and stirs the mind.

How the Gunas Shape the Mind

The gunas not only color mood. They also determine which part of the mind leads.

When Sattva predominates

Buddhi shines. Its light filters through Manas gently, keeping perception clear. Ahamkara softens, serving rather than ruling. Chitta releases old impressions easily. Actions are guided by wisdom. Even effort feels graceful. Decisions arise from understanding, not impulse.

When Rajas predominates

Ahamkara becomes loud. It borrows Buddhi's light to chase desire and defend identity. Manas over collects sensations, overwhelming the intellect with noise. Chitta fuels the race by replaying success and fear. The mind becomes sharp but unsettled, brilliant in movement and blind in stillness.

When Tamas predominates

Manas dulls, Buddhi dims, and Chitta sinks into confusion. Ahamkara hides behind excuses or self pity. Thought becomes slow. Reflection heavy. Willpower faint. The same faculties that once served wisdom now serve inertia. Awareness itself seems distant, though only veiled.

Understanding these inner shifts helps us respond wisely. When Rajas rises, pause and breathe before acting. When Tamas thickens, move the body, seek light, or speak truthfully. When Sattva dawns, protect it. Simplify, rest, and share its clarity with others. The gunas are not enemies. They are signals on the dashboard of the mind. By reading them rightly, we travel the day with greater harmony.

In Daily Life

Food
Sattvic: fresh fruits, vegetables, grains.
Rajasic: spicy, fried, or excessively stimulating.
Tamasic: stale, processed, or overcooked.

Lifestyle
Sattvic: moderation, simplicity, regularity, meditation.
Rajasic: competition, hurry, ambition, constant doing.
Tamasic: avoidance, overindulgence, neglect, confusion.

Mind
Sattvic: clarity, compassion, steady joy.
Rajasic: craving, comparison, restlessness.
Tamasic: apathy, denial, ignorance.

Even small choices, food, company, or entertainment, shift the balance of these energies. Life is a field of continuous influence. Awareness is the gardener.

Why Serenity Needs Sattva

Serenity is not something we create. It is the natural fragrance of the Self. But the mind must be pure enough to reflect it.

- A Sattvic mind is like a still lake that mirrors the moon perfectly.
- A Rajasic mind is like water in constant waves, the reflection breaks and scatters.
- A Tamasic mind is like a muddy pond, the moonlight cannot even enter.

Thus, cultivating Sattva is not the final goal, but it is the essential beginning. Sattva brings light to Rajas and motion to Tamas, guiding both into harmony. When Sattva prevails, Buddhi shines, Manas calms, and Ahamkara softens its grip.

Parable: The Three Lamps

In a hall, three lamps are lit.

- The Sattvic lamp burns steady and bright, revealing everything clearly.
- The Rajasic lamp flickers, sometimes dazzling, sometimes blinding.
- The Tamasic lamp smolders, barely lighting the room.

The Self is the same flame shining through all three. Only the clarity of the lamp differs. If the flame wavers, we do not blame the light. We simply steady the lamp. So too, peace is not absent. The mind just needs to become still enough for its light to shine.

A Quiet Pause

There are days when the mind feels light,
as if a window opened inside
and fresh air moved through everything.

And there are days when the same mind feels heavy,
as if a curtain has been drawn
across the inner sky.

These shifts can feel mysterious,
but beneath them moves a quiet rhythm,
the rise and fall of energies

we call the gunas.

Sometimes clarity spreads like morning sunlight.
Sometimes restlessness beats like midday heat.
Sometimes heaviness settles like dusk
and everything turns inward.

Yet beneath all of it
there is a steadier ground,
something that does not change
even when the mind does.

If we sit for a moment,
we can feel that ground waiting,
like cool earth under fallen leaves.

Thought may swirl.
Emotion may surge.
But a small part of us
is already watching.

Quiet.
Unmoved.
Aware.

Let attention rest there for one breath.
Not to escape the weather,
but to remember it is only weather.

The gunas may color the moment,
but they do not define us.

Reflection for the Reader

Sit quietly for a moment and turn your attention inward. Notice the movement of your own day and how your inner weather has shifted from morning to evening.

Think of one recent moment when your mind felt light and clear.

What were you doing just before that?

And think of another moment when heaviness settled in. What small choice pulled you into that mood without you realizing it?

Recall a simple act from today that brought restlessness, or a simple act that brought ease. Let your awareness move through these small scenes gently, as if watching your own life from a little distance.

Now ask yourself: What quality was strongest in me today, the clarity of Sattva, the drive of Rajas, or the heaviness of Tamas?

Not as a judgment, but as a quiet observation.
How did the food you ate, the sleep you had, or the company you kept shape these states?

Can you remember a time, even recently, when you felt naturally clear, light, and content without effort?
Notice how real that clarity felt, and how easily it fades when the mind is pulled outward.

Finally, place your attention on one simple thing that brings more Sattva into your life. A quiet morning. A sincere word. A moment of kindness. A gentle breath before speaking.

. . .

These are not dramatic acts. They are small, luminous gestures that open the heart to clarity. Sit with that recognition for a moment and feel how simple choices shape the inner world.

Closing

The gunas are not abstract philosophy. They are the texture of daily life. They shape how we see, how we respond, and how close or distant we feel from our Self. To observe the gunas is the beginning of understanding them. As we live with more awareness, the movements of Sattva, Rajas, and Tamas become a gentle teaching in themselves.

- A Sattvic mind brings peace and clarity.
- A Rajasic mind brings effort and growth.
- A Tamasic mind brings rest, but if prolonged, it turns into heaviness.

Our task is not to judge these movements, but to understand them. By observing these inner tides, we learn when to act, when to pause, and when to simply be. As this understanding grows, it naturally begins to shape the roles we live each day.

If you are a mother, you may notice moments of impatience soften as you recognize the rise of Rajas and gently nourish the calm of Sattva. If you are a father, you may bring steadiness to your children as you sense when Tamas weighs you down and shift toward clarity. If you are a partner, you may listen with more openness, aware of how your inner state colors every moment. If you are a spiritual seeker, your practice may deepen as you see that the gunas are movements of nature, not flaws in who you are. If you are a worker, an artist, a leader, or a student, your focus and creativity may grow naturally as Sattva becomes more familiar.

Whatever your path, the same serenity begins to express itself through your actions, quietly and steadily. The gunas do not define who you are. They only color the mind through which you look. When these colors settle, the clarity of the Self shines naturally.

PART I SUMMARY: THE HUMAN CONDITION

In the first part of this book, we stayed close to what every person can recognize without theory. We began with the fog: that familiar feeling that life is moving, yet something inside remains unclear. The world may look fine from the outside, but within, there can be restlessness, repetition, and a quiet dissatisfaction that does not go away through quick fixes. The sages never called this a personal failure. They treated it as a human starting point, the place where a real journey begins.

From there we turned toward the instrument through which this fog is experienced: the mind. We saw that the mind is not the enemy. It is a mirror. When it is steady and clean, life is seen with simplicity and truth. When it is stirred by fear, desire, and old impressions, the same life looks distorted. We also saw that the mind is not one voice. It is an inner orchestra, with different functions working together. When they cooperate, clarity returns. When they pull in different directions, the fog thickens and we become reactive without realizing why.

Then we looked at the threads that color this inner world from moment to moment. The sages named them the gunas: clarity, motion, and heaviness. These are not moral labels. They are the shifting weather of the mind. They explain why the same person can feel open and clear in the morning, restless at midday, and dull by night. Understanding this movement gives us compassion. We stop treating moods as identity. We begin to see them as passing forces that can be noticed, balanced, and guided.

Together, these chapters form a single insight. Much of what we call suffering is not caused by life itself, but by how life is filtered through a mind that is clouded, pulled, or tired. When we begin to notice the fog, understand the mirror, and recognize the gunas, something changes. We do not immediately become perfect. But we begin to become less confused about why we suffer, and less helpless inside our own patterns. We begin to stand on firmer ground.

And this naturally raises a deeper curiosity. If these same patterns shape our inner world so precisely, what about the outer world. If clarity and distortion are not random in us, is the universe also moving by a design we can understand. Is there an order beneath what looks like chaos. Is there a larger intelligence behind the rhythms of life, the rise and fall of experience, and the strange unevenness of human paths.

That is why Part II begins. We move from the inner landscape to the wider canvas. Not to escape personal life, but to place it inside a bigger view. We step from the psychology of the mind into the architecture of nature itself, from the individual fog into the larger pattern in which all experience appears.

PART TWO
THE STRUCTURE OF REALITY

CHAPTER 4

THE HIDDEN WHOLE

MAYA AND THE UNITY BEHIND DIVERSITY

Why the Mind Needs a Story

The restless mind seeks a vast framework. The sages offered a cosmic story to steady perception. When we look at the night sky, something inside falls silent. The same stars our ancestors saw still shine above us, yet we rarely pause to notice. The mind is restless. It circles around small worries. Why me. Why this. Why now.

Without a framework, it keeps spinning, trying to make sense of fragments. The sages understood this. They offered not commandments, but a story, a map for reflection. A story wide enough for the mind to rest upon. When we hold a cosmic picture, our personal storms shrink to size. A broken day becomes one ripple in a vast ocean. This is not escape. It is perspective.

Brahman Alone Is

Before time ticked its first second, before matter took shape, before thought arose, there was only Being. Not a thing or a person, but the silent fact of existence itself.

The sages named it **Brahman**.

Sat: the fact that something is
Chit: the light by which it is known
Ananda: the fullness that needs nothing added

Everything else, body, breath, thought, galaxy, rises and falls within that one field, like waves upon an ocean. The waves move. The ocean remains. Brahman is like sunlight before there were windows to enter, mirrors to reflect it, or eyes to see it.

Then comes the natural question.

- If reality is changeless and whole, why do we see a world of change and conflict.
- Why does perfection seem to fragment into opposites like gain and loss, birth and death.

The sages replied softly. Reality has not changed. Our vision has. When the mind is restless, reality appears broken. When it becomes still, the same world shines with harmony.

Just as a lake reflects the moon perfectly when calm but breaks its image when disturbed, what we call world is our reflection of the infinite. Even in nature, perception depends on the instrument. An eagle, with its sharp eyes, sees patterns hidden from us. A dog, guided by scent, lives in another dimension of signals. If humans had an eagle's sight or a dog's nose, our world would not look the same. So what we experience as the world is not fixed. It is a projection through our senses and mind. When these instruments quiet down, the picture clears. Order replaces chaos.

Maya: The Creative Veil

To explain this mystery, the sages spoke of maya. Not illusion as falsehood, but the lens that projects the One into the many. It is the unseen screen upon which the movie of life unfolds. Without the screen, no picture could appear, yet the screen itself is untouched by every scene.

Maya is like a crystal prism placed before a beam of white light. The light is single and colorless, yet as it passes through, it appears as many colors. Each color is real in its own way, yet none exist apart from the white light.

So too, Brahman does not change, yet through the prism of maya, it expresses as everything, from the movement of galaxies to the beat of your heart. The same power that veils the Self when the mind is restless also reveals it when the mind becomes still. The sages called that interplay the play of maya.

The Threefold Manifestation

When the sages looked deeply into the nature of existence, they saw that the One reality expresses itself in three ways, without ever becoming three. Just as electricity expresses as light, heat, and movement depending on the instrument, consciousness expresses differently depending on the lens of maya.

This is not mythology. It is a map of how the One appears as the many, and how the many remain rooted in the One.

1. When sattva dominates maya: the order of the whole (Isvara)

When the quality of clarity rises in maya, consciousness appears as the quiet intelligence that permeates everything. The sages named this Isvara, but they did not mean a deity sitting somewhere outside creation.

They meant:

- The precision of natural law
- The symmetry in mathematics
- The unfolding of a seed into a tree
- The intelligence in the structure of DNA
- The rhythm of breath and heartbeat
- The balance of ecosystems
- The moral arc of human conscience

This is the cosmic mind, the total intelligence in which all individual minds appear like waves in a single ocean.

The ancients expressed this poetically, but it is the same insight modern science edges toward when it speaks of unified fields, elegant equations, emergent order, and the fine tuned nature of the universe. It is not a person. It is order itself, the harmony that allows life to exist and persist.

2. When rajas dominates maya: the individual point of experience (Jiva)

When the quality of movement predominates, the same consciousness appears as the countless centers of experience we call individuals.

This is Jiva, not just a human being, but consciousness functioning through a particular body-mind lens, shaped by tendencies, impressions, conditioning, desires, and fears.

Each Jiva experiences a particular world through its own form and nature, yet all are rooted in the same universal consciousness. This is why living beings seem separate, though the light behind them is one. Each Jiva is like a unique window, but the sunlight entering through all windows is the same.

3. When tamas dominates maya: the world of matter (Jagat)

When inertia thickens in maya, consciousness takes on form, solid, structured, measurable. This appears as matter. From stars to oceans, from mountains to molecules, from the body to the brain, matter is consciousness in its most condensed expression.

The sages never meant that matter is unreal. They meant matter is the furthest condensation of the same reality that shines as mind and intelligence. Just as water becomes steam, liquid, or ice depending on temperature, consciousness appears as:

- pure awareness (Brahman)
- mind and experience (Jiva)
- form and substance (Jagat)

The substance is one. The expressions are many.

Macro and Micro: One Canvas

The vast and the intimate follow the same design. The same cosmic rhythm flows through the human mind. Prana connects the universe and the individual through a single quiet movement.

- When sattva shines in us, buddhi becomes clear. The mind reflects the harmony of the larger intelligence.
- When rajas surges, ahamkara and manas leap outward, grasping, reacting, claiming.
- When tamas thickens, dullness and confusion spread and the instruments grow heavy.

Through all of this, prana keeps steady rhythm. Inhale, pause, exhale. Creation, sustenance, and dissolution. Macrocosm and microcosm breathe together.

Parable: The Lamp and the Shadows

A single lamp burns in a quiet room. On one wall the shadow is sharp, on another it flickers, and on a third there is none. The lamp does not choose. It simply shines. What stands before it determines how much light appears. Light never changes. The mind's coverings decide how much reaches through.

- When the covering is thin, light passes. This is sattva.
- When movement scatters it, shadows dance. This is rajas.
- When coverings grow dense, darkness appears. This is tamas.

The lamp has not changed. This is maya at play.

The Seed and the Tree

Within a seed sleeps the entire tree, with roots, trunk, branches, and fruit. Given warmth and water, it bursts open in creation, grows and holds through sustenance, and finally returns to the soil in dissolution. Nature repeats this rhythm everywhere.

- Thoughts rise, hold, dissolve.
- Days begin, unfold, fade.
- Lives emerge, mature, and return.

To see this pattern is to glimpse the order behind apparent chaos.

Seeing Through Maya: Reflections, Dreams, and Projections

Maya is not distant or abstract. It operates within every act of perception. Each time consciousness turns outward, a world appears and is experienced.

A mirror offers the first clue. Stand before it and the reflection moves exactly as you do, yet it is not you. The image borrows its life from the original and vanishes when you turn away. In the same way, the world borrows its appearance from consciousness. Nothing exists apart from that awareness, yet everything seems separate until the source is remembered.

A still lake reveals this again. When calm, it reflects the sky perfectly. When disturbed, the image breaks into fragments. The lake has not lost the sky. Only its stillness. So too, when the mind quiets, reality is seen clearly. When restless, it distorts the reflection and calls it the world.

The sun and its rays offer another image. The rays appear many, touching every surface, yet there is only one sun. Awareness is one, though appearing through countless experiences. When we follow each ray back to its origin, unity becomes clear.

Dreams bring the truth even closer. Within a dream, a whole world arises with people, rivers, and sky, all sustained by the dreamer's own mind. When the dream ends, nothing was lost. It was never outside the consciousness that dreamed it. Waking experience follows the same principle. The universe exists only as it is known within awareness.

A screen and projector reveal the play of maya. Light passes through the lens, and instantly the world appears. Storms gather, lovers meet, children laugh, battles unfold, seasons turn. A lifetime of emotion flickers across the surface. Yet through every scene, the screen remains untouched.

On that silent expanse,
summer fields shimmer,
winter rains fall,
autumn leaves drift,
and spring blooms return.
Cities rise, empires fade,
waves crash, mountains sleep,
and still the screen does not change.

- Consciousness is that screen.
- Maya is the projecting power.
- The drama of life is the moving picture.

The play seems real because the light moves quickly, story after story flowing in seamless succession. But when the projection pauses even for a breath, only the screen remains, whole, unchanging, serene.

To know this is not to reject the movie. It is to watch without fear. The storms do not stain the screen. The fires do not burn it. The tears do not soak it. The joys do not bind it. The screen sustains them all and remains free. Every experience rises like rain upon the surface of a lake and dissolves back without leaving a mark. The screen does not choose the scenes. It simply allows light to play upon it.

This is the mystery the sages saw. The world is a story of shifting shadows. The Self is the unmoving ground beneath them. When this is known, life continues, but its weight disappears.

Every moment of life repeats this pattern. Waking brings creation. Thinking sustains it. Sleep folds it back into silence. Each morning's world is a small act of creation. Each night's rest is a quiet dissolution. The same intelligence that moves galaxies shapes the rhythms of a single day. Maya is not an enemy to escape. It is the mirror through which the infinite learns to see itself.

Why the Sages Told This Story

The creation story is a medicine for restlessness. Understanding replaces confusion with wonder. The sages offered this story for a simple purpose, to steady the mind.

In the earlier chapters we saw how the fog of ignorance blurs perception, how the mind reflects or distorts the Self, and how the gunas color every movement of awareness. Now those same threads are seen not only within us, but woven into the universe itself.

The mind cannot leap from confusion to truth in a single stride. It moves through understanding, first noticing patterns, then sensing harmony, and finally resting in silence. The cosmic story makes this journey gentle. It gives the intellect a map, the heart a sense of belonging, and the senses a horizon wide enough to quiet their wanderings.

It is like a child waking from a bad dream. A parent offers a soft story, not to create another fantasy, but to calm the fear so the child can awaken fully. In the same way, this story soothes a deeper unease, the quiet ache of not knowing where we belong.

Once the mind is calm, it can glimpse what lies beyond all stories. Even a brief vision of this order changes how we live. The world feels purposeful. Action feels natural. Suffering becomes part of learning rather than a personal burden. The fog that once seemed dense begins to glow from within, lit by a truth that does not come and go.

A Quiet Pause

There are moments
when the world suddenly feels wider
as if something in the heart remembers
that life is more than this small circle of thought.

Maybe it happens under a night sky
when the stars seem ancient and familiar
like old teachers who have been waiting for you to look up.

Maybe it happens at the ocean
when the waves rise and fall
with a rhythm older than memory
and something inside begins to follow their breath.

In those moments
the mind loosens its grip
and the world stops feeling like a puzzle
that must be solved.

Instead
it becomes a vast unfolding
full of light and shadow
movement and stillness
held together by a single quiet intelligence.

The many shapes of life
begin to feel like colors of one light
and for a breath
you sense the presence behind all forms
the stillness beneath all change
the witness behind every experience.

This glimpse is not imagination.
It is recognition,
the remembrance of something you have always known
but often overlook in the noise of the day.

Let that spaciousness touch you again,
not fully,
just enough for the heart to open by one soft degree.

Even a moment of this seeing
makes the world feel less heavy
and more like a beautiful play

unfolding on a screen that never moves.

The forms will keep shifting,
but the one who sees remains clear,
quiet,
untouched.

Reflection for the Reader

Think of a moment from your life that felt larger than you. Maybe a childhood night under the open sky, or the first time you saw the ocean, or a moment of loss or wonder when the world felt strangely vast and intimate at once. Hold that memory for a breath.

Notice how something inside shifted. Thoughts paused. The heart softened. Worries stepped aside. In that brief opening, you sensed a wider story, even if you did not have words for it. That quiet recognition is the same glimpse the sages pointed toward when they spoke of maya and the One behind the many.

Ask yourself gently. When I look back at all the versions of myself across the years, who is the one who has been watching them. When moods rise and fall, when beliefs change, when my world expands or contracts, what in me remains unchanged. In moments of silence, when there is no past to defend and no future to chase, what is it that feels quietly present. If all the forms in my life come and go, what is the space in which they appear.

Let these questions rest without trying to solve them. Sit for a moment with whatever feeling rises. Notice the simple fact that you are here, aware and present. This awareness does not come and go with your moods. It does not age with your body or tire with your thoughts. It is the same light that has been with you since the beginning, steady behind every change.

Carry this noticing into the next few moments of your day. Let it soften the way you see yourself and the way you see the world. The many forms will continue to shift, but the one who sees remains quietly whole.

Closing

The story of creation is not history. It is a medicine for the restless mind. It reminds us that behind every motion lies stillness, behind every form lies the formless, and behind the many lies the One. Maya continues its play, yet the fear of the play begins to soften. We live, act, love, and rest with a quieter heart, knowing that everything appears within a single, unbroken wholeness.

When the insight of this chapter settles even a little, when we sense that all forms arise within one reality, life begins to feel simple again.

If you are a mother, patience begins to arise without effort. If you are a father, steadiness and warmth grow more naturally. If you are a partner, you listen more fully. If you are a spiritual seeker, your practice feels more grounded as the play of maya becomes less threatening and more transparent. If you are a worker, an artist, a leader, or a student, your effort gains quiet precision and care.

Whatever your role, serenity begins to move through it, softly and steadily, giving ordinary moments a gentle radiance. In that rhythm, peace takes root.

From this peace, a natural question appears. If the underlying reality is one and harmonious, why do human lives unfold so differently. Why does one person meet ease while another meets struggle. What subtle law shapes the pattern of our days.

The sages called it karma, the architecture woven by every thought, word, and action. This is the principle that guides our next chapter.

CHAPTER 5

THE ECHO OF ACTION

THE LAW OF CAUSE AND EFFECT

The Uneven Landscape of Life

Some lives begin in ease, others in effort. One person seems to glide through fortune while another struggles against every wave. Why such a difference? If the same intelligence breathes through all, why are our paths not the same?

The sages never said that life is fair by human standards. They said it is precise. Nothing unfolds outside the quiet law that keeps life in balance. This law is called karma, the subtle current that connects cause and effect across both the visible and the invisible. It does not punish or reward. It simply restores balance wherever imbalance appears, the way gravity returns a tossed stone to the ground.

When we look at another's joy or pain, we see only the surface. Behind it flows a longer story, shaped by actions, intentions, and impressions carried through time. Each life is a chapter in a book the soul has been writing for ages. A child's kindness that grows into lifelong generosity, a careless lie that ripples into mistrust, an act of courage that opens unseen doors, these are not coincidences. They are continuations.

Every thought, word, and action plants a subtle impression in the mind, like a seed waiting for the right season to sprout. A kind act strengthens the tendency toward kindness. A harsh one strengthens restlessness or fear. Over time, these impressions shape our character and the circumstances we meet. What we call fate is often the flowering of earlier choices, seen and unseen.

So the question *Why me?* softens into *What now?* The focus shifts from blame to learning. Karma is not a sentence. It is a classroom. Every experience, pleasant or painful, is a lesson showing where the mind still clings or resists. When this is understood, life stops feeling arbitrary. The uneven landscape begins to reveal a pattern, one that quietly guides the traveler toward balance.

This brings us to a deeper truth the sages pointed to: balance is not imposed on life from outside. It arises naturally, the same way nature restores itself when left to its own rhythm.

The Subtle Balance of Life

If we watch nature long enough, we begin to see how balance maintains itself. A forest burns and new life sprouts from the ash. A wave crashes and the sea smooths itself again. Nothing is wasted. Nothing is without consequence.

So it is in human life. Every thought, word, and action sets something in motion, and that motion eventually returns. Karma is this self-adjusting rhythm of existence. It is not a judge in the sky. It is the intelligence that keeps order within the dance of life. When the mind is restless, it calls this justice or fate. When it is clear, it sees only harmony, each effect perfectly matched to its cause.

Think of a musician tuning an instrument. If one string is too tight, the melody strains. If another is loose, the song falters. Living is constant tuning, guided by feedback from experience.

Pain is not punishment. It is information.

Joy is not reward. It is resonance.

This balance is working quietly all the time. We meet people who mirror our tendencies, face events that echo hidden desires or fears, and are drawn into circumstances that complete lessons left unfinished. Life often teaches through reflection rather than through blunt reward or punishment.

Karma does not chain us to the past. It connects us to learning. When awareness enters an action, the loop begins to loosen. We still act, but we see, and seeing changes everything. The same deed done unconsciously binds, while the same deed done consciously begins to free.

To live in tune with this law is not to withdraw from action. It is to act with understanding. When we recognize that every choice carries weight, we choose with care, and that care itself becomes freedom.

To see this more clearly, we need to understand what karma truly is, not as destiny or fate, but as action and the impressions it leaves behind.

. . .

The Meaning of Karma

Karma simply means action. It includes not only what we do with our hands and words, but also what we think and intend in the quiet space of the mind. Every movement of energy, whether physical, emotional, or mental, leaves an imprint. These impressions become the seeds of future experience.

The sages said:

Sow a thought, reap an action.
Sow an action, reap a habit.
Sow a habit, reap a character.
Sow a character, reap a destiny.

Destiny is not imposed on us. It is grown by us. Each moment we plant new seeds, and each day we harvest the fruits of earlier ones.

The teaching describes three broad categories that shape our journey:

- **Sanchita karma** is the stored past, the total collection of impressions lying dormant in the field of the mind.
- **Prarabdha karma** is the portion of that storehouse which has ripened into the circumstances of our present life, including the body we inhabit, the family we were born into, and the broad contours now unfolding.
- **Agami karma** is the new seeds we plant today through action, intention, and thought, shaping what is yet to come.

Imagine three arrows. One has already left the bow, one is being aimed and drawn, and countless others lie waiting in the quiver.

The archer cannot stop the arrow already in flight, but he can choose where to aim the next. This is the quiet hope hidden in karma. We cannot rewrite the past, but we can transform the present, and through the present shape the future.

To understand how these seeds take root and influence our lives, we must look more closely at the inner soil in which they are planted.

The Cycle of Inner Seeds

Within us lies a subtle field where every action takes root. When we act with strong emotion or intent, the energy of that moment condenses into an impression (*samskara*), a faint trace left upon the mind. These impressions gather in the storehouse of memory (*chitta*) and gradually shape the patterns of our thoughts, emotions, and behaviors. The teaching describes this inner cycle as a quiet chain moving within us.

1. **Samskara** is an impression. Every experience leaves a mark. Joy, fear, anger, kindness — each creates an imprint waiting just beneath awareness.

2. **Vasana** is a tendency. When similar impressions repeat, they gather strength and turn into leanings of personality, the subtle pulls toward certain actions, reactions, and choices.

3. **Vritti** is a thought-wave. When a tendency rises to the surface, it becomes a thought, a ripple on the mind that shapes how we interpret what is in front of us.

4. **Kama** is desire. A thought we identify with becomes: *I want.* Desire focuses the mind and pulls energy in a particular direction.

5. **Trishna** is craving. Desire that hardens turns into restlessness and attachment. The mind becomes bound to its object and loses balance.

6. **Karma** is action. Craving pushes us to act, and every action plants fresh impressions, restarting the cycle.

So the wheel turns:

samskara → vasana → vritti → kama → trishna → karma → samskara

A living loop of creation, turning quietly within us, shaping habits, moods, and the path of our lives.

The sages said, "As the seed, so the fruit." A vasana, when the right soil appears, germinates. That seed becomes a vritti. The thought, if nourished, becomes desire. Desire ripens into craving. Craving compels action. Action leaves another seed, completing the circle.

Consider a simple example. You once admired a beautiful car. The image, touched by emotion, became an impression. Later, when a neighbor bought the same car, that old impression stirred into a thought: *I want it too.* Desire arose. Perhaps comparison followed, planning or striving, until action completed the circuit. Outside, it looked like a small event. Inside, the mind was reliving its own projection. When understanding enters, the pattern begins to loosen. Desire no longer commands. Awareness begins to choose.

Or consider a time when someone's comment hurt your feelings. The sting became an impression and settled quietly within. Later, when another person said something similar, that old impression stirred into a thought and quickly colored your reaction. What felt like a new irritation was simply an old seed sprouting again. When this is recognized, the loop loosens. You are no longer reacting only from the past, and a new level of freedom begins to appear.

To see how these seeds shape our inner life, we have to look at the instruments within us that receive, interpret, and store every experience.

The Role of the Inner Instruments

Each part of the inner mechanism we explored earlier plays a distinct role in shaping how impressions form and how actions arise.

- **Manas**, the mind, gathers impressions from the senses. It receives the raw data of experience, the sights, sounds, and feelings that enter through the outer world.
- **Buddhi**, the intellect, evaluates and guides. It asks the essential questions: *Is this right? Is this needed?*
- **Ahamkara**, the sense of "I," claims ownership. It says, *I want this* or *I did that,* weaving experience into identity.
- **Chitta**, memory, stores impressions for future recall. It holds the seeds of past experiences, waiting for the right moment to surface.

When these instruments work in harmony, the mind becomes clear. Buddhi guides, manas listens, ego cooperates, and memory rests until it is needed. When ego overrules buddhi or memory stirs old cravings, the current of action becomes clouded and the cycle of impressions tightens.

. . .

Think of a phone camera with a smudged lens. The scene in front of you is the same, but the picture looks unclear. A simple wipe reveals that nothing outside was the problem. The lens only needed attention. In the same way, when the inner instruments are steady, life becomes easier to understand. When they are clouded, even simple moments feel confusing. Many of the difficulties we face are not flaws in the world but smudges on the inner lens.

Freedom is not gained by stopping action. It is gained by refining the source from which action arises. Two people may perform the same deed. One becomes bound through attachment. The other grows freer through selflessness. Karma depends not only on what we do, but on the intention and awareness with which it is done.

And because every action arises from a particular inner state, the teaching points to one more influence shaping the nature of karma: the three gunas moving through the mind.

The Gunas and Karma

Every action arises from a particular state of mind, colored by the three gunas: **sattva**, the quality of clarity; **rajas**, the quality of restlessness; and **tamas**, the quality of inertia. The nature of our karma depends on which of these qualities is strongest at the moment of action.

Think of it like the different performance modes of a phone. Sattva is when the phone runs smoothly and efficiently. Everything responds clearly, and even complex tasks feel manageable. Rajas is like having too many apps open at once. The device heats up, drains energy, and performs with strain. Tamas is low-power mode, when the screen dims, speed slows, and even simple actions feel heavy. The same phone is there throughout, but its state determines how well it functions. In the same way, the guna active in the mind shapes the quality of our actions.

- **When sattva is present**, action becomes a clear stream. The mind feels calm and steady, and work flows without strain. Even difficult tasks are done with a quiet joy. Such action refines the mind and leaves little residue behind.
- **When rajas dominates**, the mind begins to push and strive. Action comes from desire, comparison, or the need to prove something. It may bring achievement but not always peace. Rajas fuels movement, ambition, and creativity, but it also strengthens the sense of *I am the doer* and often leaves behind excitement, fatigue, or frustration. Rajas is not negative. It simply needs direction and balance.
- **When tamas prevails**, clarity fades. Action becomes careless, sluggish, or harmful. It may come from confusion, avoidance, or wrong intention. Tamas binds deeply because it feeds misunderstanding and drains inner strength. Its fruit is heaviness, dullness, or regret.

We move through these states every day. Morning may feel light and clear. Afternoon may bring restlessness. Evening may settle into fatigue. The gunas shift like weather in the mind.

When sattva rises, nurture it gently.
When rajas surges, channel it into meaningful work without clinging to outcome.
When tamas thickens, shake it off with movement, breath, or reflection.

Karma yoga, the practice of action with awareness and without attachment, is the art of balancing these gunas. Duties are done sincerely but without craving or aversion. Action continues, yet the sense of bondage loosens. Life itself becomes the training ground for freedom.

To understand how these states shape our journey more deeply, we turn next to the movement of action itself and how each deed plants a seed for the future.

The Cycle of Action and Reaction

Every action is a seed. Some sprout quickly, some lie dormant for years, and some never grow because the soil is no longer fertile. But every seed carries the potential to bloom when the right conditions arise.

Just as a gardener tends the soil, we tend the field of our mind. Whatever we plant, whether kindness or anger, generosity or fear, will return as fruit. The seed forgets nothing. It only waits for its season.

We may remember a moment from school when embarrassment took root while speaking in front of others. The moment was small, but it left a seed. Years later, as an adult, the same person may feel sudden anxiety before a presentation without knowing why. The situation is new, but the inner seed is old. When the right conditions appear, the seed awakens, not to punish, but to reveal what still needs understanding and release.

This is how karma works. An action filled with emotion or attachment plants a subtle seed in chitta. That seed, a samskara, may germinate in this life or another, when the right people, place, and situation bring it to the surface. No act disappears. It simply waits for its time.

The sages compared this to a farmer's field. A farmer sows grain but does not expect harvest the next morning. He knows that time, rain, and sunlight must cooperate before the seed breaks open and grows. So it is with karma. The fruit, or *phala*, ripens only when cause, condition, and opportunity align. The law is not mechanical. It is intelligent, rhythmic, alive.

Karma expresses itself through the conditions of its age. An intention, once sown, waits until the right soil appears. When it ripens, it finds expression that matches the era, the environment, and the instruments available. A person who once longed for swift travel might have received a horse and carriage. The same karmic tendency today may bring an electric car or a plane ticket. The seed is the same — the desire for movement — but the fruit adjusts to the age in which it matures.

This shows that karma is not a rigid law of reward and punishment but a living intelligence. It responds to *kala* (time), *desha* (place), and *patra* (circumstance). The soul evolves, and the instruments of expression evolve with it. Only the inner tendency, the vasana, travels forward, seeking fulfillment until it learns what it needs to learn.

The sages told a simple parable about this. A man once shouted angrily into the hills, and the echo returned the same harsh tone. Later, filled with joy, he called out again, and the echo came back soft and sweet. He realized the hills were not judging him. They were returning his own voice.

. . .

So it is with karma. Whatever energy we send in thought, word, or deed returns when the time is right. Sometimes quickly, sometimes after long seasons, but always in harmony with the pattern we ourselves created.

Within this moving cycle, awareness becomes the gentle pause, the space where a new direction becomes possible.

The Role of Awareness

Awareness is the gentle pause in the wheel, the space between cause and effect. It is the moment where the old pattern can stop and a new direction can begin.

Imagine anger starting to rise. In the first flash of awareness, you can see it forming, a spark before the flame. If you watch it carefully, without feeding it, the spark dies on its own. If you react to it, it becomes a fire that burns both ways, creating new seeds. Awareness is the difference between compulsion and freedom. The more present we are, the more consciously we participate in our own evolution.

A simple example makes this clear. Someone says something sharp, and the familiar rush of irritation appears. In an unconscious moment, the reaction would be immediate. But if awareness steps in, even for a breath, the energy shifts. The same situation becomes a chance to understand rather than to react. The outer moment has not changed. Only the inner stance has.

Karma binds only when it is unconscious. Awareness loosens its knot. When we act with clarity, seeing each situation as an opportunity for learning rather than reaction, the seed of karma burns in the fire of understanding. Its momentum exhausts itself without leaving residue. This is why the sages compared wisdom to fire. It consumes even heavy impressions when they are met directly and understood.

Reflection turns reaction into response.
Service turns selfishness into strength.
Acceptance turns fate into freedom.

Karma is not a prison. It is a curriculum. Each experience arrives as a lesson perfectly suited to our growth. If we resist, the lesson returns in another form. If we understand it, we graduate from it.

The sages told a simple parable. A farmer stored two baskets of seeds. One he locked away, fearing loss. The other he sowed in open soil. When the rains came, the stored seeds decayed, while the planted ones grew into nourishment and shade.

So it is with karma. Actions hoarded in fear or selfishness stagnate in the mind, growing into heaviness and confusion. Actions offered freely, with sincerity and openness, blossom into nourishment for the heart.

With awareness, karma stops feeling like a chain and begins to feel like a teacher. The same patterns that once bound us become pathways to clarity.

Freedom Within Karma

Karma is not a burden. It is a school. Every experience, joyful or painful, returns to balance what was once disturbed. If we resist, the lesson repeats. If we learn, the cycle completes. This is why awareness transforms karma faster than effort alone. Actions done in unconsciousness multiply the web. Actions done in clarity begin to untie it.

Our past shapes the field of experience, but it does not confine what we may become. The law of karma is not fatalistic. It is dynamic compassion. It offers endless chances to rediscover harmony.

The chain of cause and effect is vast, yet not unbreakable. Karma binds when the sense of "I" claims ownership of every action, the feeling that *I act, I control, I deserve.* The moment that claim softens, freedom begins.

We may work late on a project and feel unappreciated. Without awareness, the mind immediately creates a story: *They don't value me.* That story becomes frustration. Frustration becomes withdrawal. Withdrawal becomes new karma. But if awareness enters, even briefly, the same moment becomes lighter. You still do the work, but without the inner burden. The outer action is identical. The inner experience is transformed. The chain weakens because the ego is no longer holding it so tightly.

The teaching does not ask us to stop acting. It asks us to act without bondage, to live fully yet lightly, to move through duty and relationship with a soft understanding: *I am not the doer; action simply flows through me.* This shift changes everything.

When work is done for personal gain, ego tightens. Every success inflates pride. Every failure hurts. When the same work is done as contribution, without clutching the result, the heart stays light. Effort remains, but anxiety fades. This is the essence of karma yoga, action offered with sincerity and without attachment. A mother feeding her child, a doctor treating a patient, a student learning with focus — each can live this truth without withdrawing from the world. The secret lies not in what we do, but in how we hold it inside.

The Inner Alchemy

Inside every action lies a quiet opportunity; a moment where something automatic can soften and something new can open. This is the inner alchemy of karma, where reaction slowly becomes understanding.

When an emotion rises, whether anger, jealousy, or impatience, awareness lets us see the movement before it becomes a story. Anger often hides something it wants to protect. Jealousy often sits on top of an unspoken longing. The moment we notice this, the energy that once pushed us into old patterns begins to loosen.

In daily life, this shift can be simple. A message arrives with a tone that feels harsh, and the familiar surge appears. Yet if awareness steps in even for a breath, the moment becomes clear. The reaction was not only about the message, but about an old echo stirred within. The same energy that could have become conflict now becomes insight. Nothing outside changed. Something inside understood.

A child spills something just as the mother is rushing. The sharp *Why now?* rises. She catches it, takes one breath, and the moment turns into: *It's okay, we'll clean it.*

. . .

A short reply from a manager lands like criticism. The mind starts building a story. He pauses, rereads it later, and sees it was feedback, not rejection. The heat drops, and the next step becomes clear.

An artist stares at the page and feels the urge to force something. He notices the tightness, steps away for a few minutes, and returns softer. The next line comes without strain.

In each case, the outer action remains simple, but the inner stance shifts. The heart grows lighter. The mind becomes clearer. Action becomes nourishment instead of pressure.

Every action has this dual possibility. When it is driven by craving or fear, the mind tightens and the chain of karma grows heavy. When it is approached with sincerity, with a sense of offering rather than grasping, the same action becomes freeing. The outer task does not decide the result. The inner chemistry does.

As sattva grows, desire turns into offering, effort turns into service, and ordinary moments take on a quiet grace. Slowly, life stops feeling like a series of pressures and becomes a field of learning. Even difficult moments lose their sense of punishment. They become part of a larger movement returning us to balance. Nothing is wasted. Everything instructs.

The ego, once loud, becomes quieter. Action continues, but the noise around it fades. The witness, calm, aware, and steady, begins to appear. This is the beginning of true freedom.

. . .

The sages expressed this through a simple story. A young archer practiced daily, proud of his precision. One day a master watched him and said, "Your aim is sharp, but your mind trembles with every gust of wind."

The boy replied, "Then I must wait for the wind to stop."
The master smiled. "No. You must learn to breathe with it."

Karma is like that wind. It cannot always be predicted or controlled. But we can learn to breathe with it, to move with life rather than against it. When we do, the arrow flies not from tension, but from stillness.

A Quiet Pause

There are days when life feels like a long chain of causes and effects.
One thing leads to another, words ripple into consequences,
and the mind quietly wonders if anything is ever really in our hands.

Yet somewhere beneath all this movement,
there is a small, steady space that does not rush.
A pause before a word is spoken,
a breath before a reaction hardens,
a softness that appears just long enough
for a new choice to be born.

Not everything is fixed.
In the middle of the pattern,
there is always a place where you can see,
even for a moment,

what you are about to repeat
and what you are ready to release.

Sit with that space for a while.
It may be small,
but it is already freedom in seed form.

Reflection for the Reader

Take a quiet moment and look back over the last few days of life. Notice one situation where you felt caught in a familiar pattern. Perhaps it was a recurring argument, a feeling of being overlooked, or a habit you return to when you are tired or stressed.

Gently ask yourself:

What was the seed underneath this pattern?
Was it a fear of not being seen?
A desire for control?
An old hurt that still echoes?

Now recall a moment, even a small one, when you became aware in the middle of a reaction. Maybe you paused before sending a message, softened your tone in a conversation, or chose to listen instead of defend.

How did that tiny shift change the experience?
How did it feel inside your body and mind?

Consider one area of your life where you can bring this awareness more consciously.

What would it look like to treat your daily experiences not as rewards or punishments, but as a curriculum designed for your growth?

If each situation is a lesson, what is life gently trying to teach you right now?

Let the questions settle without rushing for answers. Often understanding appears quietly, like a seed breaking open beneath the surface.

Closing

Karma is not a distant law sitting in judgment over our lives. It is the intimate pattern through which our own thoughts, intentions, and actions return to us, again and again, until understanding dawns. When seen only from the outside, it can appear harsh or mechanical. When seen from within, it begins to feel like a patient teacher, repeating a lesson until it is truly learned.

As awareness grows, the chain that once felt heavy starts to loosen. The same experiences that once seemed random or unfair begin to reveal a simple logic. Where we clung, life brings opportunities to release. Where we avoided, life brings opportunities to face. Where we acted unconsciously, life brings chances to act with clarity. Slowly, karma stops feeling like something happening to us and starts to feel like a path that is walking with us.

. . .

When this understanding deepens even slightly, it naturally begins to show in daily life.

If you are a mother, you may find yourself responding to your children with more patience, seeing each difficult moment as a chance to plant a different seed. If you are a father, you may bring steadier warmth to your family, noticing where old reactions can soften into new responses. If you are a partner, you may listen more openly, recognizing how past impressions color present conversations and choosing not to let them rule the moment. If you are a spiritual seeker, you may begin to see your challenges not as obstacles on the path but as part of the path itself, each one shaping your understanding. If you are a worker, an artist, a leader, or a student, you may discover that intention matters as much as outcome, and that offering your effort lightly brings a new kind of ease to your work.

Life does not become perfect. It becomes transparent. The same actions, when approached with awareness, lose their heaviness and gain meaning. What once felt like a closed loop of fate begins to open into a living dialogue between you and existence.

This is the promise at the heart of karma rightly understood. Not a sentence, but an invitation. Not a fixed destiny, but a field where every moment offers a chance to plant a different seed.

As we begin to see karma in this way, another layer of understanding quietly invites itself forward. If karma shows the continuity of experience, a natural question arises: what keeps this experience moving moment to moment? What breathes life into the body, animates thought, stirs emotion, and carries awareness through every action?

The sages pointed to a hidden current flowing through all living things. They called it **prana**, the subtle force behind every movement of life. In the next chapter, we turn to this unseen rhythm that flows within us, shaping every breath, sensation, and feeling. It is the movement beneath all movements, the life within life.

CHAPTER 6

THE FLOW WITHIN

THE UNSEEN RHYTHM BEHIND ALL MOVEMENT

The Breath of Life

There is a rhythm moving through all things, tides that rise and fall, winds that travel from sea to land, the pulse that beats within every creature. And yet, many days do not feel rhythmic. They feel noisy inside. Thoughts jump, emotions pull, energy rises and drops without warning. It can feel like an instrument that is technically working, but not in tune.

Many of us know this feeling. A day begins with a rushing mind, a phone full of messages, a small worry that grows, and before we notice, even breathing becomes tight. Nothing dramatic happened, yet we feel inwardly strained, as if life is playing too fast.

The sages did not treat this as a personal failure. They pointed to a simple truth. Life is moved by a subtle current, and when that current is scattered, our inner world becomes scattered too. They called this current prana, the breath of life, the quiet force linking the seen and the unseen. Air is what we breathe. Prana is the living current we feel moving through breath, through attention, through vitality. We may not see it, but we can sense its presence by its effect.

We do not create prana. We participate in it. Each inhalation draws in the universal force, and each exhalation offers it back. It is the same current that makes sap climb a tree, carries clouds across the sky, and moves thought through the mind. When this current flows steadily, the body feels lighter and the mind feels clearer. When it becomes blocked or wasted, heaviness, confusion, or fatigue can appear even when we cannot explain why.

Breath is the visible face of this invisible power. If prana is the current, then breath is the place where we can feel it directly. It is like the mouthpiece of an instrument, the one part we can actually touch. That is why the sages called breath a bridge between body and awareness. By sensing breath, we begin sensing prana. And by sensing prana, we begin to return to rhythm.

Pause for a moment and feel one natural breath, its cool entrance and its gentle exit. In that small cycle, the whole story repeats, receiving, holding, releasing. What looks ordinary is not ordinary at all. The same pulse that turns galaxies turns within the chest. To recognize this is the beginning of pranayama, not as control, but as learning to cooperate with the intelligence already breathing through us.

The Hidden Current

Behind every visible motion lies an unseen mover. A thought rises, an emotion stirs, a hand lifts, yet beneath them all runs one subtle current, prana. We often mistake activity for energy, but activity can be frantic and still leave us empty. True energy is quieter. It supports movement without scattering itself.

We can sense this in the simplest way. Some days we wake up and everything feels usable. Attention holds. Effort feels clean. Even challenges feel manageable. Other days, the mind feels like it is buzzing. The body feels heavy. Even easy tasks feel like pushing through mud. The sages would say the difference is often not the size of our problems, but the condition of the inner current moving through us.

In the language of the sages, prana expresses itself in five main ways, called the pancha pranas. These are not ideas to believe. They are ways the sages mapped what we can observe within ourselves. We can think of them as five winds inside one instrument, each wind doing a different kind of work.

1. **Prana** is the inward and upward current, linked with breathing and the heart area, drawing life inward.
2. **Apana** is the downward current, linked with elimination and grounding, helping us release and stabilize.
3. **Samana** is the balancing current around the navel, linked with digestion and distribution, helping things settle and harmonize.
4. **Udana** is the rising current, linked with speech, expression, growth, and lift in the system.
5. **Vyana** is the circulating current, spreading through the whole body, linking everything together like a network.

For example, when we feel the body releasing and settling, apana is doing its work. When digestion and balance return after food, samana is active. When speech rises cleanly, udana is present. These names help us notice what was already happening.

. . .

When these five move in rhythm, the instrument plays well. The body becomes steady. The mind becomes clear. When they move out of rhythm, life feels off. Sleep becomes irregular, appetite shifts, thoughts repeat, emotions jump. Nothing is "wrong" in the moral sense. The inner winds are simply not coordinated. And this is what pranayama is for, not as a performance, but as a return to coordination.

Breath as Mirror

Breath is not only a doorway into prana. It is also a mirror of mind. When thoughts race, breath becomes shallow. When fear rises, breath tightens. When peace appears, breath softens like a quiet stream. This is one of the most direct mirrors we have.

We can watch it in daily life. In a tense conversation, breath becomes quick and uneven. While listening to music, sitting near the ocean, watching a sunset, breath slows, deepens, and widens. The sages kept pointing to this because it makes the teaching usable. We may not be able to command the mind, but we can work with breath. We can soften the exhale, and the mind often follows.

It is like an instrument again. If the airflow is harsh, the sound is harsh. If the airflow is steady, the sound becomes smooth. In the same way, if breath is jagged, the inner world feels jagged. If breath becomes steady, the inner world begins to settle.

Every mood has its breath. Anger runs hot and fast. Worry becomes tight and restless. Sadness becomes heavy and sinking. Love expands the chest. Fear contracts it. When awareness enters breathing, these moods stop being rulers. They become weather passing through a larger sky.

A few conscious breaths do not remove life's events, but they change the field in which events are held. This is not escape. It is return.

The Four Movements of Breath

The sages noticed that each breath carries a complete pattern. It is not just in and out. It is like a short musical phrase with a beginning, a fullness, a release, and a rest. They named these movements:

- Inhalation (puraka) is receiving.
- Retention (kumbhaka) is holding and stabilizing.
- Exhalation (rechaka) is releasing.
- Stillness (shunya or bahya kumbhaka) is resting after release.

These are not only physical actions. They are metaphors for life. We receive experiences, we hold and digest them, we release what we can, and sometimes a quiet space appears after letting go. That space is easy to miss when we live in speed, but it is precious. It is where the mind stops grabbing, even if only briefly.

When breath is disturbed, the rhythm becomes rushed, and life feels rushed. When breath becomes heavy, the rhythm becomes dull, and life feels dull. When breath returns to natural rhythm, something inside begins to feel musical again. Not in a poetic sense only, but in a practical sense. The inner world becomes less chaotic.

The Practice of Harmonizing Energy

Pranayama is not forcing breath. It is the art of tuning. The sages approached it the way a musician approaches an instrument, by listening first. Not demanding a sound, but restoring rhythm.

It can begin very gently. Eyes closed, attention notices the breath as it is, short or long, warm or cool, even or uneven. Nothing has to be judged. Nothing has to be fixed right away. The simple act of noticing often softens the breath on its own, as if breath responds to being met. And if strain appears, the breath is allowed to return to normal. Gentleness comes first.

A few simple supports can help, kept simple and gentle.

- Rhythm can be noticed without judgment, because the mind steadies when it feels safe.

- The places where breath rushes or hides can be noticed, because breath often reveals where tension lives.

- The exhale can be allowed to lengthen naturally, because a full exhale releases residue like a wave drawing back to sea.

- A small pause after exhale can be welcomed, because rest is part of rhythm.

- The inhale can be allowed to rise by itself, because trust restores what control breaks.

Over time, the breath becomes smooth. The mind becomes clearer. The body becomes lighter. Not because we conquered something, but because resistance loosens. When breath is uneven, thought scatters. When breath flows like music, thought settles.

. . .

How This Connects to What Came Before

Everything we learned earlier converges here. We explored the mind and how it reflects or distorts reality. We explored the three gunas, clarity, activity, and inertia. Now we meet a living bridge underneath those ideas, prana moving through breath.

When breath is uneven, rajas and tamas tend to rise, and restlessness or heaviness fills the mind. When breath steadies, sattva rises, and perception brightens. This is why breath practice belongs to every path. It gives us a direct handle on the inner climate.

Karma also meets us here. In the earlier chapters we saw how actions leave impressions, and how those impressions return as moods, reactions, and repeating patterns. Prana is the current that carries that momentum moment to moment. When this current is scattered, old tendencies rise faster and we act on impulse. When it steadies, a small space opens between impulse and response. In that space, karma stops being automatic and begins to become conscious.

The sages also pointed to something deeper. Maya projects the world of form, but prana animates it. Prana is the connecting thread between the vast and the intimate. To breathe consciously is to remember that we are not separate from the larger movement. The outer and the inner are not two. They move together as one current.

A Quiet Pause

There are days when everything feels slightly out of tune.
The body is here, the mind is moving,
but the inner rhythm feels uneven.

Yet somewhere beneath all this motion,
there is a small, steady space that does not rush.
A pause after letting go,
a breath before a reaction hardens,
a softness that appears just long enough
for a new choice to be born.

Not everything is scattered.
In the middle of the day,
there is always a place where you can feel,
even for a moment,
what you are about to repeat
and what you are ready to release.

Sit with that space for a while.
It may be small,
but it is already peace in seed form.

Reflection for the Reader

Take a quiet moment and look back over the last few days of your life. Notice one situation where you felt scattered, heavy, or unusually reactive. Perhaps it was a tense conversation, a day of rushing, or a moment where a small thing felt bigger than it should have.

Gently ask yourself:

What was happening to your breath in that moment?
Did it tighten?
Did it rush?
Did it become shallow?

Often breath tells the truth before the mind admits it. Now recall a moment, even a small one, when you softened in the middle of a reaction. Maybe you paused before replying, took one slower exhale, or chose to listen instead of defend.

How did that tiny shift change the experience?
How did it feel inside the body and inside the mind?

Consider one area of life where you can bring this awareness more consciously.

What would it look like to treat breath like a tuning key, not as a technique, but as a way of returning to rhythm when you drift?
If the inner instrument is slightly out of tune, what is one simple way you can bring it back?

Let the questions settle without rushing for answers. Often the understanding appears quietly, like a seed breaking open beneath the surface.

Closing

Prana is not a concept we have to believe in. It is the subtle current through which life moves the body, steadies attention, and carries the mind from moment to moment. When prana is scattered, we feel scattered. When it is balanced, we feel balanced. Breath is the simplest doorway into this truth, because breath is where we can feel the current directly.

As awareness grows, life begins to feel less like noise and more like rhythm. We recover faster after stress. We notice tension earlier. We respond with a little more space. The outer world may not change, but the inner tempo becomes steadier, and that steadiness changes how life is experienced.

When this steadiness deepens even slightly, it naturally begins to show in daily life. If you are a mother, you may find more patience in your care, because the breath is no longer feeding urgency. If you are a father, you may bring calmer strength to your actions, because the inner tempo is steadier. If you are a partner, you may listen with more openness, because breath creates space before reaction. If you are a spiritual seeker, you may stop chasing experiences and begin trusting the quiet depth that is already present. If you are a worker, an artist, a leader, or a student, you may discover that a calm breath changes the quality of effort itself.

Life does not become perfect. It becomes more rhythmic. And when rhythm returns, something in us recognizes its own home. Breath continues, life continues, yet within every movement there can be peace. The sages pointed to this peace again and again, not as an idea, but as a presence we can learn to feel.

If prana is the moving current, we naturally begin to wonder about the knower of the current, the awareness that remains steady while breath and mind move. If breath is a wave, what is the ocean that holds every wave?

As we begin to sense prana more clearly, another layer quietly opens. Breath shows us that life is not only a series of outer events. There is an inner momentum moving underneath, carrying moods, tendencies, and impressions forward from moment to moment. A single breath can change the mind, and a single pause can loosen a reaction. This hints at something larger.

The movements within us do not simply vanish when a moment ends. They continue until they are understood.

This is where the sages take the conversation further. If a pattern can repeat through a day, and if desire can return again and again until it settles, what happens to that momentum when the body itself comes to an end? Does it disappear, or does it seek another form?

In the next chapter, we look at the turning wheel, the continuity of consciousness, and how the law of karma continues its movement until understanding brings it to rest.

CHAPTER 7

THE TURNING WHEEL

BIRTH, DEATH, AND THE RHYTHM OF RETURN

The Continuity of Consciousness

When an action sends its echo through time, the echo does not always end inside one lifetime. The movement continues as long as its momentum remains. Life and death, in this view, are not final breaks in the process. They are pauses in one continuous flow of awareness, like a wheel that disappears behind a wall for a moment and then reappears still turning.

A single lifetime is often too short for the seeds we plant to fully ripen. Some lessons unfold slowly. Some desires take time to settle. Some impressions need a wider canvas. When their results cannot complete themselves here, the movement continues, seeking expression in another form. Rebirth, then, is not separate from the law of karma. It is the same current of cause and effect unfolding across a longer span of time.

Rebirth is not meant as a belief we force onto ourselves. The sages presented it as the natural extension of continuity. Just as a story rarely fits into one chapter, consciousness moves through different frames of experience to complete what remains unfinished. Death is not an ending. It is a doorway. Day gives way to night and night to dawn, yet the light remains the same. In this way, awareness moves through cycles of appearance and withdrawal, carrying momentum forward.

The sages call this turning rhythm ***samsara***, the wheel of birth and rebirth. It is not described as punishment. It is described as process, consciousness evolving through form, remembering itself little by little. And if consciousness continues in this way, a natural question arises. What guides that continuity from one life to the next, and what exactly is it that continues.

The Law Behind Rebirth

Every birth arises from causes already set in motion. Karma, the quiet law of cause and effect, carries forward whatever remains unfinished. It does not assign a new beginning from outside. It simply continues the movement already underway, like a wheel that keeps spinning when the hand has pushed it.

The sages said nothing in us is lost. The impressions we create, the desires we nurture, and the tendencies we strengthen continue even when the body falls away. These tendencies are called ***vasanas***, inner leanings that quietly shape what we are drawn toward and how we respond. We may not remember the earlier moments that formed them, yet we can feel their pull in the present.

The body dies, but the inner traveler does not end with the body. The mind, carrying memory, longing, and momentum, moves onward. The sages used gentle images to help us feel this. One lamp lights another without losing its flame. In the same way, consciousness shifts from one form to another, continuing the story that could not finish in a single chapter.

A simple image makes this clearer. Imagine a musician switching instruments. The violin may break, but the music does not end. The musician picks up a new instrument and continues the song from where it paused. The instrument changes, but the momentum of the melody remains. Rebirth, in this sense, is not a dramatic leap into another universe. It is consciousness returning to a new setting where unfinished lessons can unfold naturally.

And if life continues in this way, we naturally wonder what happens in the quiet space between one instrument and the next.

Between Two Lives

Between death and birth, the sages describe a subtle interval, not as a final heaven or hell, but as a pause in the great classroom of existence. It is a space of review, rest, and quiet assimilation, where the impressions of the last life settle and the outline of the next life begins to take form.

We can think of a traveler who finishes a long journey and rests for a night before setting out again at dawn. During the rest, experiences settle, the nervous system becomes quiet, and direction becomes clearer. Rest does not end the journey. It prepares the traveler for what comes next.

So too in this interval. The tendencies we have cultivated rise closer to the surface, forming seeds of future experience. Whatever seeks completion moves forward. Whatever has fulfilled its purpose falls away. It is not a courtroom. It is not a reward hall. It is simply the meeting place where the momentum of the past and the possibilities of the future gather themselves into a life suited to the soul's next steps.

This is why the sages spoke about rebirth with calmness. It is not meant to make us afraid. It is meant to make life more intelligible. If the wheel keeps turning, it is because something within keeps pushing it. And that brings us to the most practical part of this teaching: how the push weakens, and how the wheel begins to slow.

Breaking the Cycle

The wheel of action continues as long as something within us keeps turning. Old impressions rise again. Unfinished desires look for expression. The story continues from one scene to the next. What we call another life is simply the continuation of lessons that were not yet complete.

Understanding is what gently slows this movement. The moment we truly see a pattern, the energy that once fed it begins to lose strength. A man who reacts in anger for years suddenly notices the anger rising before it spills into words. In that single moment of seeing, a space opens, and the old rhythm weakens.

Someone keeps trying to be liked, to be praised, to be seen. Then one day it becomes clear: the real hunger is not approval. It is peace. In that moment of seeing, the grip loosens. The same life continues, but the pressure drops, because the push behind it has changed.

These small recognitions become turning points. A single insight can dissolve what once seemed to require another lifetime. This is why the sages compared samsara to a potter's wheel.

The wheel spins quickly as long as the hand keeps pushing. The moment the hand lifts, the wheel begins to slow. Samsara works in the same way. When unconscious desire pushes the mind, the cycle continues. When awareness removes the push, the wheel naturally comes to rest.

Rebirth continues only when momentum remains. When the mind becomes clearer, the need for repetition fades. Consider a simple example. Someone who has always felt jealous of a sibling suddenly sees that the emotion is not hatred but a longing to feel valued. The insight does not erase the past, but it loosens the knot that kept the pattern alive. What could have repeated again and again begins to end in a breath of understanding.

This is how the cycle begins to break, not through harsh discipline or dramatic renunciation, but through gentle and honest seeing. Awareness loosens what effort alone cannot touch. As the mind becomes steadier, the heart grows lighter, and action loses its compulsion.

The sages call this ***moksha***, liberation. It is not escape from the world. It is the clear recognition of the Self, where the sense of bondage ends at its root. Birth and death belong to the body. Learning and forgetting belong to the mind. The Self remains untouched by both.

A metaphor the sages often returned to is the dream. In a dream everything feels real. Yet the moment we wake, nothing holds us. The scene dissolves, but we remain exactly as we are. Liberation is this quiet waking, not a journey to another world, but a recognition of the awareness that has always been here.

The wheel turns until understanding appears. When understanding is steady, the movement ends. When the mind becomes clear, the soul rests in its natural freedom.

A Quiet Pause

Between two thoughts there is a small quiet.
Between two breaths there is a soft space.
Between two lives, the sages say, the same quiet exists.

In that space nothing is demanded.
Nothing must be solved.
Nothing needs to be carried forward.

It is simply a resting place.

A place where the old loosens its grip
and the new has not yet begun.

Sometimes this pause appears in daily life too.
A moment of clarity after confusion.
A breath when a pattern stops repeating.
A tenderness that rises for no reason at all.

These small openings are the same doorway that ends the cycle of return.
The mind may travel through many lifetimes, but the Self is always here.

Reflection for the Reader

Take a quiet moment and look at the movements within your own life. Notice if there is a pattern that feels older than the present moment, a fear that reappears in different situations, a longing that keeps returning, or a tendency that shows up even when outer circumstances change.

Gently ask yourself :

What momentum might be behind it?
Is it an old impression that never found closure?
Is it a desire that keeps seeking expression?
Is it a habit that has gathered strength over many years and now rises almost automatically?

Now recall a moment when you recognized a pattern as it was happening. Perhaps you caught yourself before reacting in a familiar way. Perhaps you understood why a certain emotion felt deeper than the situation itself. Perhaps you sensed that something inside you was repeating an old rhythm.

How did that recognition feel. Did it soften the moment?
Did it create a little space within you?

Consider one place in your life where this awareness could be brought more consciously.

What would it look like to meet that tendency with understanding instead of habit?
If each experience is part of a longer journey, what lesson might this moment be inviting you to see?

Let these questions rest gently. Understanding does not always arrive loudly. Sometimes it appears like a small shift inside, the beginning of a pattern loosening, the first sign that the wheel is slowing of its own accord.

Closing

Rebirth is not offered as a distant doctrine. The sages described it as the quiet continuity through which our own tendencies return to be understood. What repeats is only what remains unfinished. What loosens through awareness does not need to return. When we see this, life feels less like a random path and more like a gentle unfolding of lessons meant to bring us toward clarity.

As understanding grows, the wheel that once felt relentless begins to slow. The same events that once felt heavy begin to reveal their pattern. Where we clung, life gives chances to release. Where we avoided, life gives chances to face. Where we acted unconsciously, life gives chances to act with awareness. Slowly, what looked like fate begins to feel like learning, and what felt like a chain begins to feel like a teacher.

When this understanding deepens even slightly, it naturally begins to show in daily life. If you are a mother, patience may rise more easily, because the old urgency no longer drives every moment. If you are a father, steadier warmth may guide your actions, because you are no longer pulled by the same hidden pushes. If you are a partner, you may listen more fully, noticing when the past is trying to speak through the present. If you are a spiritual seeker, challenges may feel less like punishments and more like invitations to see clearly. If you are a worker, an artist, a leader, or a student, even ordinary effort can feel lighter when it is no longer fueled by compulsion.

Life does not suddenly become perfect. It becomes transparent. The same patterns that once repeated begin to loosen. The same inner knots that once demanded another round of learning begin to dissolve. This is the quiet promise the sages point to: freedom is not something we manufacture. It is something we uncover, one honest insight at a time.

And as this becomes clearer, another question naturally rises in us. If the wheel turns through the momentum of the mind, what is it that witnesses the wheel. What is the steady presence that remains while experiences change.

PART II SUMMARY: THE STRUCTURE OF REALITY

In Part II, the sages help us see life from a wider altitude. What looks like a scattered world begins to reveal a hidden order. We start by looking at maya, not as a trick, but as the power that makes the One appear as many. Diversity is real at the surface, yet beneath it there is unity. This view does not erase daily life. It softens the confusion that comes when we treat appearances as the whole truth. When we remember the hidden whole, the mind relaxes. We stop fighting life as if it is random, and we begin to sense a deeper coherence moving through it.

From that foundation, the sages turn to karma, the echo of action. Every thought, intention, and deed leaves an impression, and those impressions return as experience. Karma is not punishment and it is not reward. It is balance. It is life teaching life. When we understand this, the question "Why me" begins to soften into "What is this teaching me now." We do not become passive. We become precise. We learn to act with clarity, because action is always shaping the inner field from which the next moment will arise.

Then we move closer to what we can feel directly. The sages point to prana, the living current within, the energy that carries breath, attention, vitality, and mood. By noticing the flow of prana through breath, we begin to understand why the mind becomes restless or calm. We see that steadiness is not only a mental idea. It is a rhythm that can be felt, restored, and lived.

Finally, the sages widen the lens again. If momentum can carry itself through a day, and tendencies can repeat for years, what happens when the body itself ends. This is where the turning wheel becomes meaningful. Samsara is the continuation of unfinished momentum, and rebirth is the return of tendencies that still seek completion. The cycle does not break through force. It slows through understanding. When we truly see a pattern, the push behind it weakens. The wheel begins to slow on its own.

Part II gives us a single message in different forms. Life is not random. It is patterned. Maya explains why the world looks divided. Karma explains why actions return. Prana explains how momentum moves inside us. Samsara explains why momentum continues until it is understood. And through all of it, the sages keep pointing us back to the same quiet promise. Freedom is not something we invent. It is something we uncover, one clear insight at a time.

Part II has widened our view. It has shown us the hidden order behind what once felt random, and the quiet laws that shape how life appears and repeats. But seeing the structure is not the same as being free inside it. Understanding can explain the wheel, yet we still have to live our days while the wheel is turning.

That is where Part III begins. Here the sages turn from architecture to application, from explanation to inner transformation. We move into the practices that refine the mind, soften the heart, steady attention, and make insight livable. Not as techniques for a "spiritual life," but as a way for the modern mind to become clear, stable, and whole in the middle of ordinary life.

PART THREE
THE PATH OF CLARITY

CHAPTER 8

THE FOUR PATHS

ONE DAILY RHYTHM

THE FOUR PATHS: ***Action, Devotion, Stillness, and Understanding***

There are times when we understand something clearly, yet we still cannot live it. We can see the pattern of our own mind. We can even name it. But when the day speeds up, when emotions rise, when life presses in, we fall back into what is familiar.

This is not because we are insincere. It is because habits are strong. Understanding is like seeing a map of a mountain trail. The map can be accurate and still our legs must walk. The terrain still has slopes. The weather still changes. The body still gets tired. Wisdom has to become practice before it becomes steady.

This is where practice enters the journey. It is not a new belief, but a way of living what we already recognize. The sages called this Yoga, not as escape from life, but as integration inside life.

Why Many Paths Were Taught

Human beings do not open through the same doorway. Some of us are led by inquiry. We want clarity first, or we feel lost. Some are led by love. The heart softens before the mind understands. Some are shaped through work and responsibility. Service becomes their teacher. Others are drawn inward. Silence steadies them more than explanation.

The sages noticed this and did not force one method onto every temperament. They offered four main paths, not as competing roads, but as harmonized disciplines of life.

- **Jnana Yoga**, the path of inquiry and understanding
- **Bhakti Yoga**, the path of devotion and love
- **Karma Yoga**, the path of selfless action
- **Raja Yoga**, the path of stillness, meditation, and inner mastery

Each is a doorway that leads toward the same recognition, the Self beyond the restless mind. These names are not meant to make life complicated. They are meant to make inner movements memorable. Sanskrit words act like signposts. They help us point to realities that are otherwise hard to describe.

But a doorway is meant to be entered, not clung to. When we make one approach the whole house, the journey can tilt. We see this in ordinary life. Understanding without warmth can become dry, like light without heat. Love without discernment can become attachment dressed as devotion. Work without inner quiet can become restless, like a wheel that never stops turning. Stillness without returning into life can become withdrawal, calm on the surface but closed at the edges.

Yoga is not about choosing a personality. It is about balance, blending insight, devotion, work, and stillness into one living rhythm until life begins to feel integrated.

The teaching calls this harmony Integral Yoga, the alignment of head, heart, hands, and spirit. It is not an escape from the world. It is learning to meet the world without losing the center.

The Logic Behind the Practices

Many people come to practice for a simple reason. Something hurts. The body feels tight. The mind feels restless. Sleep is shallow. The heart feels heavy. So we try something that seems to help. A few stretches. A few quiet breaths. A few minutes of sitting. Relief comes, and we are grateful, but often we still do not know what truly changed inside.

The sages gave a deeper explanation. They said we live through instruments. The body is one instrument. Breath and prana are another. The mind is another. And the sense of I, the doer and the owner, is another. When these instruments are out of tune, life feels noisy even when life is fine. When they begin to align, the same life feels lighter, clearer, and more stable.

This is why practice works. Not as superstition, and not only as health improvement, but as inner tuning. When the body becomes steadier, it can hold stillness without strain. When breath becomes steadier, prana steadies, and the mind becomes less scattered. When attention becomes steadier, thoughts lose some of their grip. When the heart softens, the ego loosens. When action becomes offering, the weight of doership begins to fade.

. . .

The outer form can look ordinary, a posture, a breath, a mantra, a pause, a question. But the inner effect is precise. It changes the instrument through which we experience everything. That is why the same person can face the same day and yet live it differently, not because the world changed, but because the inner stance changed.

When we understand this, practice stops being something we do only when a symptom rises. It becomes something we do because we understand the human system. We begin to practice with intelligence, not blind repetition. We do not just follow instruction. We know what each practice is touching within us, and why it restores balance.

This is what the four paths are for. They are four ways of tuning the same human instrument until understanding becomes lived experience.

The Fourfold Harmony

A simple image appears again and again in the yogic map. Life is like a chariot drawn by four horses. If one pulls too hard or another falls behind, the ride becomes rough. The chariot still moves, but it sways, strains, and loses direction. When all four move together, the journey becomes smooth and purposeful.

So it is with the four yogas. They are not meant to compete. They are meant to complete one another. Each refines a different instrument within us, and each protects the others from becoming distorted.

Jnana refines clarity. Bhakti refines feeling. Karma refines intention in action. Raja refines attention and inner steadiness.

Together they shape a complete human being, wise in thought, tender in heart, balanced in action, and steady in silence.

Jnana Yoga

Jnana Yoga begins in a very ordinary place: the moment we stop and notice, something feels off inside. We might be doing fine on the outside, but the inner noise keeps running. So a simple question appears, not as philosophy, but as a way to steady ourselves:

Who am I right now, beneath this mood, this pressure, this story.

This path is not about collecting ideas. It is about learning to see clearly, the way we wipe a smudged lens so the same world looks sharper.

A helpful image is a movie screen. The scenes keep changing, a win, a loss, a compliment, a worry. But the screen itself does not change. Jnana Yoga is learning to notice the screen, not just the scenes. Thoughts still come, but we stop treating every thought like a command.

The sages called this **Viveka**, discernment. It simply means we learn to tell the difference between what is moving and what is steady.

The angry email

An email arrives with a harsh tone. The mind immediately says, They disrespected me. Heat rises. Fingers want to type fast. Jnana Yoga is the small pause that notices: This is anger showing up. It is not the whole truth. In that pause, the message is still there, but we respond more cleanly. The reaction does not drive the wheel.

The social comparison

We see someone's success online. The mind quietly tightens. I am behind. I am not enough. Jnana Yoga is noticing: This is comparison. It is a wave, not an identity. We do not need to fight it. We just stop giving it full authority.

The "I am not good at this" story

We make one mistake, and the mind turns it into a full sentence: I always mess up. Jnana Yoga is recognizing the jump: one event became a permanent label. We bring it back to truth: A mistake happened. That is all.

A simple metaphor

It is like a pair of sunglasses we forgot we were wearing. The whole world looks dark, so we assume the world is dark. Jnana Yoga is the moment we remember: Oh. This is the lens. We do not need to fix the entire sky. We just remove the lens.

In daily life, this path shows up as small honesty. We notice when a mood is trying to become a permanent identity. We notice when thought is adding extra drama. We pause and ask, Is this true. Is this needed. Is this kind. And slowly, clarity becomes more natural.

Bhakti Yoga

Bhakti Yoga refines the heart. Where inquiry purifies thought, devotion purifies feeling. Bhakti often begins with love directed toward something we experience as sacred, a prayer, a mantra, a teacher, a chosen ideal, or simply the feeling that life itself is meaningful. But the deeper movement is the same. The heart learns to soften. It learns to trust. It learns to offer rather than grasp.

Devotion is like warming your hands near a fire. You do not argue the fire into warmth. You sit close, and warmth happens. In the same way, when the heart stays close to what feels true and sacred, it softens on its own.

We can feel the difference between emotion and devotion. Emotion rises and falls with conditions. Devotion becomes a steady warmth that stays even when life is not smooth.

The Small Opening

Sometimes the mind runs all day, judging, comparing, and replaying conversations. Then something small happens. Someone is kind. A child laughs. The sky looks clear for a moment. The heart softens. For one breath, the mind stops gripping. Something in us remembers what matters.

The Breath in Traffic

Someone is stuck in traffic and the mind starts complaining. Then a small shift happens. They notice the sky, take one slow breath, and feel gratitude that they are safe and moving toward home. Nothing outside changed, but the heart opened.

One Minute of Presence

Someone is tired after a long day. A child asks for attention, or a friend calls. The mind wants to avoid. Then they pause, choose one kind response, and give their presence fully for a minute. That small offering becomes devotion in action.

As love matures, it naturally supports what the sages called vairagya, non clinging, the quiet loosening that happens when the heart stops gripping. Love becomes less about demand and more about offering. What remains is humility, sweetness, and peace.

Karma Yoga

Karma Yoga is the yoga of doing without attachment. Everyday life becomes the training ground. Work does not disappear. Duties do not disappear. The world still asks things of us. Karma Yoga simply changes the inner posture while we act.

The outer action may be the same, cooking, teaching, building, caring, managing, cleaning, supporting. But the inner grip begins to release. We act sincerely, but we stop demanding that life reward us on our terms. We do what needs to be done, and we let go of the hunger for praise, control, or constant confirmation.

This is not passivity. It is strength without tightness. When action becomes offering, ego loosens. Action continues, but bondage begins to end.

A simple metaphor

It is like carrying a glass of water while walking. When we stare at the water and panic about spilling, every step becomes tense. When we walk with care and trust our balance, the same walk becomes easier. Karma Yoga is that shift. Doing the same work, with less inner strain.

The Unseen Work

Someone cleans the kitchen after everyone eats. No one notices. The mind wants to say, Nobody cares. Then a small shift happens. The work is done anyway, but the heart releases the need to be seen. The action becomes clean. It is still effort, but it does not become bitterness.

The Result Email

Someone sends a project update and waits for approval. No reply comes. The mind starts spinning. Did I fail. Do they value me.

Karma Yoga is doing the work sincerely, then letting the silence be silence. The next step becomes clear without carrying the extra story.

The Helping Hand

Someone helps a friend move. The body is tired. The mind starts counting. I did more than they did. Then they notice the counting itself. They keep helping, but they drop the score. The same action becomes lighter.

We can sense the difference in ourselves. There is a way of working that leaves us bitter even when we succeed. There is another way of working that leaves us clean inside even when the day was hard. Often the difference is not the task. It is the attachment.

Raja Yoga

Raja Yoga is the path of stillness, inner discipline, breath, focus, and meditation. It calms the waves of thought until the lake of mind becomes clear.

This path works directly with attention and the nervous system. It teaches the mind to become steady, not by force, but by training. The sages emphasized two foundations here. Abhyasa (steady practice), returning again and again to attention. Vairagya (non clinging), not feeding every thought that tries to pull us outward. When these two mature together, stillness stops feeling like effort and begins to feel like a natural resting place.

Raja Yoga also refines prana (life force), the subtle current behind breath and mental energy. When prana is scattered, the mind scatters. When prana steadies, the mind becomes easier to gather, like a room that grows quiet when the wind stops rattling the windows.

A simple metaphor

It is like letting muddy water sit. If we keep stirring it, it stays cloudy. If we stop stirring, the dirt settles on its own and the water clears. Raja Yoga is learning to stop stirring.

The Phone Pull

Someone sits down to rest for five minutes. The hand reaches for the phone without thinking. Raja Yoga is noticing the reach. They pause. One slow breath. They do not fight the urge, they just do not follow it. The pull weakens a little.

The Before Reply Pause

Someone receives a message that feels sharp. The body tightens. Words rush forward. Raja Yoga is taking one quiet breath before replying. The same message is there, but the mind is less reactive. A better response appears.

The Night Loop

Someone lies in bed and the mind starts replaying the day. One scene repeats again and again. Raja Yoga is returning to the breath, not to fix the thought, but to stop feeding it. The thought may return, but each time they come back to breath, the loop loses fuel.

Stillness here is not dullness. It is alert quiet. It is the ability to rest in silence without boredom, and to remain present without strain. It is the mind learning not to chase every thought like a dog chasing every passing car.

When stillness deepens, awareness shines by itself. In that

stillness, understanding becomes more than thought, love becomes more than emotion, and action becomes more than effort. The four paths begin to feel like one movement.

Yoga in Daily Life

Yoga was never meant to live only in forests or ashrams. The real classroom is daily life. A conversation, a meal, a walk, even waiting in traffic can become practice when touched with awareness. The outer action may look ordinary. The inner posture makes it sacred.

We can see the four paths already moving through one day.

- When we pause before reacting, we touch **Raja Yoga**.
- When we act without needing credit, we live **Karma Yoga**.
- When we reflect before speaking, asking if it is true and kind, we apply **Jnana Yoga**.
- When gratitude rises in the middle of pressure, we enter **Bhakti Yoga**.

Everyday life is already the ashram. The goal is not to escape the noise of the world, but to find silence within it. Stillness is not absence of activity. It is presence within activity.

A mother feeding her child practices yoga when love replaces fatigue. A worker focusing on one task without distraction practices yoga through attention. A student learning for joy rather than praise practices yoga through inquiry. A stranger offering a sincere smile brings devotion into the street.

When awareness joins breath, even washing dishes can

become meditation. When gratitude joins speech, words become prayer. When service joins effort, deeds become offerings. The world does not need more retreats. It needs more awake participants.

When the Paths Tilt

Every light casts a shadow. Even good paths can drift when we lose balance. Not because the path is wrong, but because the mind clings.

• When understanding grows without warmth, it can turn hard. We may be correct but unkind. Thinking becomes a shield instead of insight. Humility brings it back.

• When devotion grows without clear seeing, emotion can blur wisdom. We may mistake attachment for devotion, or intensity for truth. Clarity steadies love, so love becomes freeing.

• When action grows without inner quiet, service turns into strain. Purpose becomes burden. We become a wheel that never stops. Stillness renews action, the way breath returns to silence.

• When stillness grows without returning to life, silence can become distance. We may pull back not from peace, but from fear of being disturbed. Gentle engagement brings warmth back.

Each path carries medicine. Each path can also become a trap when isolated. When the four are practiced together, the traps loosen. Clarity keeps love clean. Love keeps clarity human. Service keeps both grounded. Stillness keeps everything centered.

Balance does not mean perfection. It means noticing when we

are tilting, and adjusting gently, like tuning four strings by listening.

The Natural Entry Point

For each of us, one path often opens more easily than the others. Some are drawn first to clarity. Others are led first by love. Some come alive through service. Some find peace through inner stillness.

There is no hierarchy here. What comes naturally is the doorway, and the other paths arrive in time when sincerity is present, the way branches grow when the root is healthy.

A person who begins with service often discovers that service opens the heart, and the heart opens understanding. A person who begins with devotion often finds that devotion steadies the mind, and a steadier mind refines action. A person who begins with inquiry often finds that true inquiry humbles the ego, and humility opens love. A person who begins with stillness often finds that stillness brings clarity, and clarity naturally expresses itself as kindness and clean work.

We begin where we are strong, and we allow sincerity to draw the rest.

A Quiet Pause

There are days when we try to fix ourselves through effort. A new routine. A stronger will. A tighter plan.

And then there are moments when something softer happens. A breath slows. A sentence becomes kinder. A small act is offered without needing to be seen. A quiet gratitude appears for no reason at all.

In that moment we can feel the four paths meeting. Clarity, love, service, stillness. Not as separate practices, but as one life remembering its center.

Sit with that for a while. Let the day be exactly as it is. Let the heart and mind find a little alignment again.

Often the next step is not dramatic. It is simply the next breath taken with awareness.

Reflection for the Reader

Pause for a moment and look at your day. Notice how the four paths already flow through you without labels.

When you tried to understand something deeply, that was Jnana?

When you felt love without reason, that was Bhakti?

When you helped someone sincerely, that was Karma?

When you paused to breathe before reacting, that was Raja?

Now ask gently.

Where does my life need more harmony right now, clarity, love, service, or stillness?

Which doorway feels natural, and which one needs gentle cultivation?

What would it look like to live tomorrow as a more conscious blending of these four?

Let the answers come slowly. They may not arrive as words. They often arrive as quiet shifts in how we think, speak, and move.

Closing

Yoga often begins with effort, a routine we try to hold, a practice we attempt to return to again and again. But as understanding ripens, effort becomes rhythm. We begin to live from the center rather than chasing the circumference.

The sages called this state **samatvam** (inner balance), stillness within action. It does not mean life becomes perfect. It means we stop being thrown around inside life. This is the heart of Integral Yoga, not separation of paths, but their union in daily living.

When this balance begins to appear, it naturally shows in ordinary roles. If you are a mother, care becomes quieter and more patient. If you are a father, guidance becomes steadier and less controlling. If you are a partner, listening becomes more available. If you are a worker, effort becomes cleaner and less anxious. If you are a student, learning becomes more sincere. If you are a spiritual seeker, practice becomes simpler and more honest.

We do not become perfect. We become more integrated. The sacred and the ordinary begin to feel less separate.

. . .

And once we begin to live in this way, the four paths stop feeling like ideas and begin to unfold as living experience. We turn first to the path of the heart, where love steadies the mind and devotion softens the self. That is where our journey turns next.

CHAPTER 9
THE HEART'S TURN
LOVE THAT STEADIES

THE CALL of the Heart

A message arrives with a sharp tone. The mind begins to build a case. We read it twice, then three times. We plan the reply in our head. We win the argument before we even type.

Then something small interrupts the storm. A child laughs in the next room. A friend sends a simple kind line. Sunlight hits the floor. For a breath, the chest softens. The mind stops gripping. Nothing outside was fixed, yet something inside opened.

That opening is where the heart begins to lead. There are moments in life when knowledge is not enough. We may understand why the fog forms, how the mind works, or how karma returns as patterns, yet the heart still aches for something deeper. Reason can explain the mechanics of life, but only love gives it warmth.

This is where devotion begins. Not as ritual. Not as religion. As a quiet turn inside, a recognition that beneath thought and striving there is a longing to belong. A longing to return home to something we cannot name, yet deeply remember.

. . .

When the heart turns even a little, the same world looks different. A tree feels less like scenery and more like presence. Another person's pain feels less like a problem to solve and more like a call to care. We notice how easily we judge, and how easily that judgment can soften. A tenderness appears that does not need explanation. That tenderness is devotion. The heart remembering its source.

What This Is About

Devotion is not about adding beliefs. It is about changing the inner posture. Life stays the same, but we meet it with warmth instead of tightness. We begin to feel connected instead of alone. We begin to trust instead of gripping every outcome.

The sages described love as a bridge between the known and the infinite. The intellect can point the way, but the heart walks it. Love dissolves boundaries that logic cannot. It purifies without struggle, connects without condition, and makes the invisible feel near.

When love is awake, something practical happens. The mind that used to scatter in ten directions begins to quiet naturally. Thoughts soften. Breath slows. Awareness deepens, not through force, but through affection. What knowledge refines slowly, love can transform quickly.

Devotion does not mean worshiping a distant god. It is the recognition of sacredness in life itself, in work, in family, in breath, in silence. It is learning to look at life not as something we must control, but as something we can cherish.

The intellect asks, What is true. The heart whispers, I know how it feels when I am close to what is true. Both are needed, but devotion begins when we let the whisper guide the next step.

. . .

From Emotion to Transformation

At first, devotion can feel like emotion. A surge of feeling. A sweet ache. A tear that rises without warning. But the sages made a careful distinction. Emotion rises and falls. Devotion deepens and changes us. Emotion depends on conditions. Devotion remains even when life is not smooth.

Emotion often moves outward toward an object. Devotion turns inward toward the source. Over time, love becomes less about I love this or I love that, and more like love as a state of being, like a wave realizing it was never separate from the ocean.

This is why devotion has many faces. Sometimes it looks like gratitude. Sometimes it looks like service. Sometimes it looks like silence.

Three Simple Scenes

The Apology That Ends the Argument

Two people have been carrying a small tension for days. Nothing dramatic, just a cold edge. One simple sentence lands: "I'm sorry, I was tight inside." The mind stops building a case. The chest loosens. The relationship feels human again. Devotion shows up as humility, not emotion.

The Hospital Corridor

Someone is waiting outside a room, watching a loved one sleep, hearing machines, footsteps, quiet voices. No philosophy fits. No plan helps. The heart becomes quiet on its own. A prayer rises in any language, or no language. Not asking for control, only asking for steadiness. This is the heart learning trust.

The Kindness to a Stranger
A cashier looks tired. A driver lets another car merge. A neighbor carries something heavy. A small help is offered without announcing it. No one becomes a hero. But inside, the grip of "me first" loosens. Warmth replaces tightness. Devotion shows up as simple goodness.

Different Doors, Same Heart Turn
Across the world, people found simple ways to train the heart. Different cultures, different language, but the same movement. The heart becomes less defended, more available.

Gratitude before a meal.
Service done quietly.
Prayer in any language.
Singing that softens the mind.
Silence that feels like listening.
Time in nature that restores humility.
Forgiveness that ends a long inner argument.

Different doors, same direction.

The Many Doors of Bhakti

The sages used the word bhakti for this refinement of the heart. Love does not move through one doorway. It enters in different ways, shaped by temperament.

- Some hearts love through reverence. The vastness of the night sky makes them quiet. They do not argue. They bow inwardly in wonder.

• Some love through service. Their devotion appears in hands that help and eyes that see others as themselves.

• Some love through friendship. They speak to the divine as a close companion. Their devotion is intimacy, not distance.

• Some love through beauty. Music, art, nature, poetry. A melody becomes prayer. A color becomes remembrance.

• Some are drawn to silence. They do not speak of devotion at all. Their love is steady and wordless, like a lamp protected from wind.

None of these forms is higher or lower. Together they express one thing: the heart turning toward what is real.

Surrender Without Weakness

As devotion ripens, it becomes surrender, not submission, but trust. It is saying to life, I may not understand everything, but I can feel there is wisdom here. This surrender is not to another person. It is to the intelligence that beats the heart, moves the breath, and turns the stars. The same presence we have sensed in earlier chapters is now felt, not just understood.

Devotion softens the ego without struggle. What strict self discipline tries to achieve through force, love does quietly, like sunlight dissolving morning mist.

As love matures, it naturally supports ***vairagya***, non clinging, the quiet loosening that happens when the heart stops gripping. Love becomes less about demand and more about offering. What remains is humility, sweetness, and peace.

. . .

When Love and Understanding Unite

When love matures, it does not exclude thought. It begins to illuminate the mind rather than cloud it. What was once blind emotion becomes steady understanding. The head and the heart stop fighting.

Knowledge without love can become dry and distant. Love without understanding can lose direction. When they join, wisdom becomes human.

The sages called this ***prajna***, clear seeing touched by compassion.

They also described devotion ripening in a simple arc.

- At first it seeks, yearning for a response.
- Then it learns, seeing that what it sought outside has always lived within.
- Finally it rests, love remains but longing ends, because distance fades.

At this stage, understanding itself becomes devotion. Insight humbles the heart. Gratitude becomes natural. The fog of separation thins.

Making Daily Life Sacred

Devotion does not need temples or ceremonies. It begins in small moments, when we pay full attention with a warm heart.

Gratitude is the simplest form of it. It shifts us from "I should have more" to "I see what is already here."

Offering is the next step. We cook a meal, write an email, comfort a friend, not for reward, but as an offering of care. The action is the same. The inner posture changes.

Reflection deepens devotion. At day's end we pause, not to judge, but to see. Where did the heart stay open. Where did it close. That noticing is already purification.

Mantra can help too, not as magic, but as a rhythm that gathers scattered attention. A short prayer. A sacred word. A line of poetry. Even a simple thank you repeated with sincerity. Repetition works like gentle waves smoothing the shore of consciousness.

Presence is the heart of all of it. To walk without hurry. To eat with attention. To listen fully. These are the altars of daily life.

Bhakti is not something added to life. It is life lived with a gentler gaze.

A Quiet Pause

There are moments when the heart grows weary of explanation.
It has gathered many thoughts,
carried many questions,
and still it longs
for a warmth that thought alone cannot give.

Then devotion begins quietly.
Not with a command,
not with a grand feeling,
but like the first lamp lit at dusk,
small, steady, and full of nearness.

Not as belief,
but as tenderness.
Not as performance,
but as presence.

A breath softens.
A hidden gratitude opens like a flower at dawn.
The simplest act,
a word, a gesture, a moment of stillness,
begins to feel like an offering.

For a little while,
the need to understand gives way
to the grace of simply being near.
The heart no longer reaches outward.
It rests in a quiet sweetness
that asks for nothing more.

Stay with that softness for a while.
Let it be enough for this moment.
Love does not need to prove itself.
It only asks to be felt.

Reflection for the Reader

Pause for a moment and notice the rhythm of breath.

Ask gently.

Where in our life does love flow easily, and where does it close?

When we help or serve, do we expect recognition, or can we give more freely?

In what moments do we feel most connected, as if the boundary between ourselves and the world fades for a heartbeat.

Do not rush to answer. Simply notice.

If you wish, repeat a chosen word or short prayer softly, not as a task, but as remembrance. Let its rhythm settle into breath. Stay here for a few breaths. Devotion is not something we achieve. It is a fragrance already present when the heart relaxes.

Closing

When love matures, it no longer seeks approval or reward. It becomes quiet strength, the kind that holds without clinging and gives without measure. Devotion is not retreat from life. It is participation with awareness.

When devotion deepens, it quietly reshapes daily life. If you are a mother, care becomes worship. If you are a father, guidance becomes steadier and more tender. If you are a partner, love becomes freer and listening grows deeper. If you are a worker, an artist, or a student, effort becomes an offering. If you are a spiritual seeker, devotion becomes a gentle fire that keeps turning the heart toward the sacred.

Nothing needs to change outwardly. The inner posture changes. The sense of I do softens into I serve. Then the ordinary turns luminous.

. . .

This is the essence of bhakti. To sense the sacred not apart from life, but shining through it. When love and awareness walk together, wisdom blossoms naturally. In that union, the seeker and the sought begin to feel like one. And when devotion grows quiet enough, it naturally leads us toward stillness, where love no longer reaches outward, but rests in the silence from which it came.

That is where our journey turns next.

CHAPTER 10

THE STILL POINT

RETURNING TO STILLNESS

The Space Between Thoughts

Between two breaths, there is a pause. Between two thoughts, there is a small gap. We usually miss it because the next thing arrives quickly. Another thought. Another task. Another message. But if we slow down for even a moment, we can feel it. A quiet space that was already there, behind everything.

Most days, the surface of the mind is crowded. Worries, plans, voices, memories. The mind keeps replaying the film of life, scene after scene. Yet behind that movement lies something simpler. Not another scene, but the silent background that holds every scene.

Sometimes we touch it by accident. A brief pause while looking at the sky. A soft breath before speaking. A moment of stillness after a strong emotion passes. Nothing dramatic happens, but something inside relaxes. For a second, the mind stops gripping.

This is the doorway.

Practice begins when we stop rushing past that doorway. We start noticing the pause on purpose. We start returning to it again and again, the way we return home after being out in noise for too long.

When attention shifts from the movie to the screen, a new clarity begins to dawn. Thoughts may still come, but their grip softens. The heart feels lighter. The mind feels less tight. A quiet steadiness begins to hum beneath activity.

This is not escape from life. It is returning to its center. The outer world remains, but we begin to live from the still point within it, the calm center of the storm, where awareness can watch without struggle.

And this is what we usually call meditation. Not forcing silence, but remembering the silence that was never missing.

The Restless Mind and the Nature of Attention

The mind is like a river, always flowing toward whatever catches its light. One moment it runs toward sound, another toward memory, another toward imagination. It cannot remain still for long because attention has forgotten its source.

When awareness turns outward again and again, it loses strength. It becomes scattered, like sunlight diffused through clouds. But when the same awareness gathers inward, it becomes concentrated, alive. That gathered state is meditation.

The sages said the untrained mind is restless by nature. It jumps from one thing to the next, and it rarely stays with one moment for long. Trying to silence it by force only adds noise.

The gentler way is to watch patiently until attention begins to recognize its own motion.

This gentle seeing is already meditation. The moment we notice that the mind has wandered, we are no longer lost in wandering. Awareness does not need to fight thought. It only needs to remember itself.

Over time, the gap between awareness and thought widens. We begin to see thoughts as passing clouds rather than commands. We realize we can choose when to follow them and when to let them drift away.

Meditation is not about emptying the mind. It is about seeing clearly that we are not the mind. From that seeing arises natural quiet, not forced silence, but ease. The river still flows, but we are no longer swept by its current.

Anchors for Awareness

When we first invite the mind to be still, it often resists. It has lived long in motion and grown comfortable with noise. So the sages offered gentle anchors, simple ways to steady attention until stillness begins to reveal itself.

You can see this same idea across the world. Some people return to breath. Some return to a phrase of prayer. Some sit in simple silence. Some use a candle, a bead, a walking rhythm, or a quiet sound. The forms differ, but the aim is the same: to give attention one steady place to return, until the mind stops scattering.

The purpose of an anchor is not to control the mind. It is to give attention a place to return, again and again, until returning becomes natural.

Breath is the simplest anchor. It moves on its own, yet responds to awareness. We do not need to change it. We simply notice its rhythm, the cool air entering, the warm air leaving, and the small pause between. As breath becomes more visible, thought begins to soften.

The body is another doorway. We can sit comfortably and feel the weight of the body resting on the earth. We notice the rise of the chest, the pulse in the hands, the quiet hum of sensation. When attention touches the body without judgment, tension releases. The body becomes an ally of calm.

A mantra can also hold the mind gently. A mantra is sound shaped with awareness, a rhythm that gathers scattered attention. We choose a word or phrase that truly resonates and repeat it softly with feeling. The sound is not magic by itself. Its power comes from sincerity and repetition, the way a steady rhythm can calm a restless child.

The sages used the word ***abhyasa*** (steady practice) for this returning. Not harsh discipline, but consistent coming back. Each return strengthens attention the way repeated steps strengthen a path through grass.

We can also use simple observation as an anchor. A candle flame, the sound of rain, the sensation of heartbeat, even the feeling of air on the skin. What matters is not the object but the quality of watching. When observation becomes simpler and cleaner, without constant judging, the boundary between observer and observed begins to thin.

The sages called this ***dhyana*** (meditation), the flow of attention resting without interruption. It is not forced. It unfolds when attention becomes steady.

. . .

The Stages of Stillness

The journey inward does not happen in leaps. It unfolds like dawn, quietly, almost imperceptibly. At first the light touches only the horizon. Slowly the whole sky begins to glow.

Meditation moves in the same way, from effort to ease, from doing to being. At first we learn concentration. Attention keeps slipping away. Thoughts rise like ripples across a lake. This stage is not failure. It is settling. Each time the mind wanders and we gently bring it back, we strengthen the muscle of awareness. The ripples may still move, but beneath them, still water begins to appear.

As practice deepens, meditation becomes more continuous. Attention holds with less strain. The effort of focusing turns into quiet absorption, like a flame steady in a windless room. Thoughts still arise, but they no longer disturb the center. We begin to taste stillness as experience, not as an idea.

With time, a deeper opening appears. Awareness feels wider than focus itself. The sense of I loosens. Presence becomes spacious, silent, luminous. There is less method and more being. This is not a milestone to chase. It is a shift that comes when clinging softens.

Some days we will feel restless and other days still. It does not matter. Each sitting contributes to the unfolding. Even ten seconds of genuine awareness is meditation.

As clarity grows, we realize stillness was never something to reach. It was always here, beneath movement, behind thought, within every breath. The mind did not create peace. It simply stopped long enough to see it.

Meditation in Daily Life

Meditation does not end when we open our eyes. Its purpose is not to escape the world but to return to it with new clarity. If silence is only found on a cushion, it remains fragile. The deeper work is to let stillness breathe through ordinary moments.

We can begin by carrying small pauses into the day. Before speaking, feel one breath. Before eating, notice the fragrance and color of food. Before replying to a message, sense the space between impulse and response. Each pause becomes a doorway where awareness returns to itself.

Walking can be meditation. We feel the rhythm of each step, the touch of the ground, the balance of movement. When attention stays with step and breath, the whole world feels more alive.

Listening can be meditation. When we listen without rushing to respond, even an ordinary conversation becomes quieter. We begin to hear the silence beneath sound and the presence behind words.

Work can be meditation too. When attention merges with the act, writing, cooking, teaching, repairing, there is less sense of a separate doer. There is simply flow. Action becomes cleaner, and the mind grows less divided.

Meditation is not withdrawal. It is intimacy. It is learning to be present without control, involved without losing balance. When the heart learns to stay still even amid motion, every place becomes a place of practice.

A Simple Practice: Morning Stillness

Imagine beginning the day not with rushing thought, but with three quiet minutes of awareness. Sit comfortably, on a chair, a cushion, or the edge of the bed. Let the body settle as if gravity itself were a gentle hand guiding you down.

Close the eyes and bring attention to the breath. Not to control it, but to notice it. Feel the inhale. Feel the exhale. Thoughts may arrive, plans, worries, fragments of memory. Let them pass like clouds moving across an open sky.

With each breath, say quietly within, I am here. Not as a belief, but as recognition. Here in this breath. Here in this body. Here in this moment.

After a minute or two, let awareness widen beyond breath. Listen to the soft hum of life, distant sounds, heartbeat, the stillness between. Allow everything to be exactly as it is.

When the mind rests in this simplicity, a subtle joy can arise. Not because anything changed, but because for once nothing needed to. That joy is the fragrance of meditation. It appears when becoming pauses and being feels sufficient.

Even three minutes of such presence can shift the tone of the day. We speak slower, listen deeper, and meet life with more patience. Meditation becomes not a ritual but a rhythm, a daily remembrance that peace was never elsewhere.

A Quiet Pause

Between one thought and the next, there is a space that does not rush.
It is not loud, and it does not demand attention.
Yet it is always there, waiting like a clear sky behind moving clouds.

We do not have to force the clouds away.
We only have to notice the sky.

For a breath, let the mind be exactly as it is.
Let thought move. Let sensation rise. Let sound pass.

And feel what remains when we stop chasing.
A simple awareness. Quiet. Present. Unmoved.

Sit in that for a moment.
Not to achieve anything.
Only to remember what has been here all along.

Reflection for the Reader

Pause for a moment. Close your eyes and notice your own awareness, the quiet witness behind sound, sensation, and thought.

Ask gently.

When I am not doing anything, who am I?

What remains when thought subsides and breath settles?

Can stillness be felt, not as emptiness, but as presence?

Let the questions rest without chasing an answer. Often the pause itself is the response.

Now open your eyes and look around. The same world is here, the same body, the same day, and yet something feels lighter. Not because life changed, but because awareness returned to its center. If you wish, choose one small moment today to practice. One breath before speaking. One pause before replying. One minute of quiet before sleep. Let that be enough.

Closing

Meditation is not an escape from the world. It is a way of seeing clearly. When the mind grows quieter, the same world that once felt heavy begins to reveal a quieter order. Noise softens, thoughts slow, and life regains rhythm.

The practice may begin with effort, returning again and again to breath, body, or sound. But gradually it becomes more effortless, like coming home after a long journey. Moments of awareness begin to appear naturally while walking, speaking, or watching the morning light.

This is the sign that meditation is entering life. Peace no longer depends on posture or place. It begins to move gently through all that we do. If you are a mother, care becomes calmer and more patient. If you are a father, guidance becomes steadier and less reactive. If you are a partner, listening deepens and love grows freer. If you are a worker, an artist, a leader, or a student, focus sharpens and tension begins to fade. If you are a spiritual seeker, stillness begins to feel less like a practice and more like a home.

. . .

Whatever our role, we begin to live from stillness, not toward it. And as this stillness becomes more familiar, a deeper question naturally arises. If thoughts can be watched, who is the watcher? What is the awareness that remains even when the mind grows quiet?

That is where our journey turns next.

CHAPTER II

THE QUIET WITNESS

AWARENESS ITSELF

THE MIRROR of Awareness

There is a simple truth we often miss. We rarely see the world more clearly than we see ourselves.

The mind, as we explored earlier, is like a mirror. When it is clean and still, it reflects life with precision. When it is covered with the dust of desire, fear, or distraction, the reflection becomes distorted, and we take that distortion for truth.

Self inquiry begins when we turn this mirror inward. Instead of trying to fix every image in the mirror, circumstances, relationships, opinions, we begin cleaning the mirror itself. This is not effort in the outer world. It is gentle awareness directed toward the source of perception.

Every experience appears in awareness. We see, hear, feel, and think, but behind all these movements there is one constant, the silent witness that knows them. That witness is not a thought, not a mood, not a role. It is awareness itself, untouched, unchanging, luminous.

. . .

To discover this is not to create something new. It is to recognize what has always been present. When awareness looks back upon itself, the fog begins to lift. Thoughts may still move and emotions may still pass, yet something within remains undisturbed, a quiet knowing that simply says, I am.

The sages compared this to a lake at dawn. Even when ripples shimmer across the surface, the sky can still be reflected. As the winds calm, the water becomes clear enough to see to its depths, not because anything new appears, but because agitation ceases.

So it is with the mind. The purpose of reflection is not to control thoughts, but to see them as they are, transient patterns moving on the surface of something vast and still. Each moment of clear seeing is a moment of freedom. Not freedom from the world, but freedom within it.

The Nature of Self Inquiry

Self inquiry, in its purest sense, is not an exercise of thought. It is the art of turning attention back upon itself. It begins with one living question: ***Who am I***. Not asked to receive an answer in words, but asked in a way that quiets the restless movement of the mind.

When the mind asks sincerely, it cannot run far. Every direction it turns, body, role, feeling, idea, eventually leads back to awareness, the one who is seeing. Slowly, inquiry gathers scattered attention and points it toward its own source. It is like a flashlight long used to illuminate the world suddenly turning toward the hand that holds it.

The sages called this **Atma Vichara**, inquiry into the Self. It is not analysis, not self improvement tricks, and not repeating beliefs. It is recognition through direct experience. The perceiver and the perceived begin to feel less separate. The one who sees becomes more important than what is seen.

The inquiry often begins with small reflections. Who is the one who feels happy. Who notices the thought of sorrow. If we can watch an emotion arise and fade, are we the emotion itself.

Each question peels away a layer of identification, like mist dissolving in morning light.

In time, the practice shifts from asking to resting, resting as the awareness that remains when no question is needed. That is why it can feel like a pathless path. It is not traveled by movement. It is revealed through stillness.

To the intellect this may sound abstract. To the heart it can feel like home. Self inquiry is the gentle return to what has never been lost, the quiet recognition that the seeker, the search, and the sought are all the same light.

The Observer and the Observed

When we first begin to watch the mind, it can feel as if there are two of us. There are thoughts, sensations, emotions, and there is something behind them quietly watching. This simple act of noticing begins the transformation.

At first attention is pulled outward, chasing what is seen, sounds, people, memories, desires. But when awareness turns inward, it begins to recognize something important. The seen is always changing. The seer remains the same.

. . .

The body grows and changes. Moods shift. Ideas rise and fall. Yet the witness within has never aged. It has never moved in the way objects move.

The sages described this as the difference between clouds and sky. Clouds form, drift, and dissolve, but the sky is not stained by them. In the same way, the witness of experience is not affected by the passing play of thought and feeling.

We can practice this in a simple way. We sit quietly and observe a sensation, the movement of breath, the hum of sound, a passing thought. We notice how awareness knows it without becoming it. The thought appears, stays briefly, and fades. The awareness that knows it remains.

Gradually, we learn to live from that space. Events still pass through life, but we are less compelled to cling or resist. Joy and sorrow still visit, but we stop mistaking them for identity. The world remains vivid and alive, yet something inside has stepped out of the storm.

This is not indifference. It is closeness without confusion. When the observer becomes clearer, experience becomes more transparent. We begin to see through events, not only at them. And when the distinction between observer and observed softens deeply, what remains is pure seeing, consciousness knowing itself without division.

Tracing the Sense of I

Every thought begins with a small pulse inside, *I. I feel. I want. I should.* It slips into almost every sentence we speak, and we rarely stop to wonder who this I really is.

When we were children, we said I. When we grew older, we said the same word again. The body changed. The face changed.

Dreams changed. Yet something has been quietly saying I the whole time. Who is the constant one behind all change.

The sages did not ask for belief. They asked us to look.

We can sit quietly and notice how the mind keeps saying, I am tired, I am happy, I am thinking. Then we ask gently, who is the one aware of this tiredness, this happiness, this thought. We do not need an answer in words. We simply notice that the awareness watching these states is not tired, not happy, not sad. It simply is.

That quiet watcher is nearer than breath. It does not shout. It just sees.

When we trace the feeling of I back to still awareness, something softens. The endless stories of me, success, failure, pride, fear, begin to lose their grip. We realize we were never only the character in the story. We were also the page the story appears upon.

This is not cold philosophy. It is tenderness toward ourselves. It is sitting down with the mind and saying, you have worked hard enough. Let us rest. In that rest, the I that struggles fades, and the I that simply is begins to shine.

The Layers of Identity

Every morning when we wake, the mind quietly rebuilds the world and our sense of who we are within it. The body stretches. Sensations arise. Memories return. Names and roles fall into place: parent, partner, worker, seeker. Within minutes, the vast stillness of sleep condenses into a single idea: I am this person.

The sages saw that this identity is not false, but partial. It is like mist on a lake. It appears real, yet it hides the depth beneath.

To see clearly, we must learn to recognize the layers through which the sense of I is commonly felt.

These are not exactly the same as the inner functions we explored earlier, such as manas, buddhi, ahamkara, and chitta. Those describe how the inner instrument operates. Here we are looking from another angle, at the main layers through which identity is usually held and mistaken.

The first layer is the body. It hungers, tires, and changes, yet through every change the one who says my body remains. The body is like a garment, necessary and intimate, but not the wearer.

The second layer is emotion. Joy, sadness, irritation, affection, all rise and pass like clouds. They are movements in energy, not the sky itself. To say I am sad is to forget that sadness is being experienced. It is not the whole of what we are.

The third layer is the intellect. The faculty that reasons, plans, and judges. It organizes life, compares, names, and remembers. It is brilliant, yet it cannot grasp the awareness that observes it. The mind can describe awareness, but it cannot contain it.

The fourth layer is ego. The sense of I that claims every action. I did this. I failed that. I deserve this. It is the storyteller, sometimes heroic, sometimes wounded, constantly rewriting the script of life. It gives continuity to experience, yet it can also hide a deeper continuity that needs no story at all.

When we begin to observe these layers, body, emotion, intellect, ego, a quiet distance forms. We are not pushing them away. We are simply watching. And beneath them we begin to sense a subtler presence, something that does not come and go when moods change or when the body rests.

A simple image helps. It is like light shining through colored glass. Each layer tints the light in its own way, through vitality, feeling, thought, and self-claiming, yet the light itself remains clear. When attention shifts from the colors to the radiance, identification begins to loosen. We still feel, think, and act, but we no longer forget what we are beneath it all.

In the earlier chapters, we looked at the workings of the inner instrument, how manas gathers, buddhi discerns, ahamkara claims, and chitta stores. Here we are looking at the places where identity settles and says, this is what I am. Self-inquiry begins when we notice these identifications without rejecting them. Then the understanding gained earlier becomes inwardly alive. We begin to see that what works through these layers is not limited to any of them.

This does not remove us from life. It softens our grip. The body continues, emotion continues, thought continues, and ego continues to play its role. But beneath them we begin to sense a quieter continuity, the same awareness we have been approaching from many directions throughout this book. And as that awareness grows clearer, peace follows naturally, not the peace of withdrawal, but the peace of understanding.

Different Doors, Same Skill

Across the world, people found simple ways to train attention. Some sit quietly and follow breath. Some repeat a short prayer. Some walk slowly and keep attention on each step. Some use beads to keep the mind from drifting. Some sing. Some write a few honest lines to see what the mind is doing. Different cultures, different language, but the same inner skill: returning to the one who is aware.

Whatever the doorway, the direction is the same, attention turning back toward its source.

The Silence Behind Thought

Between two thoughts there is a pause. It may last only a heart-beat, yet in that pause awareness shines by itself. We often miss it because the next thought arrives quickly and pulls us back into the stream.

But if we stay still for a moment, we can feel it. A quiet back-ground behind noise, like open sky behind passing clouds.

The sages pointed to this silence as a doorway. It is not created by concentration. It is revealed when the mind stops chasing. When the lake of thought becomes still, it reflects clearly, not because the truth changes, but because the water no longer trembles.

Silence here does not mean the absence of sound. It means the absence of inner commentary. Even when the world is loud, traf-fic, conversation, laughter, something within can remain still. That stillness is not blank. It is alive, alert, aware. It hears sound, feels sensation, witnesses thought, yet remains untouched.

We can notice it now. We close the eyes. One thought comes, perhaps the thought I am reading. It fades. Before the next thought appears, there is a tiny gap, like space between waves. That gap is not empty. It is peace.

At first it comes and goes. But with practice we begin to recognize the silence was never missing. Only attention was elsewhere. Thoughts cannot erase awareness. They only cover it for a while.

Self inquiry is learning to rest in this silent background, shifting identity from thought to the awareness of thought. When we glimpse that space even briefly, something changes. The world still moves, but the center is still.

The sages used the phrase ***shanta atma***, the peaceful Self. It does not have to be earned. It only has to be remembered. And remembrance begins simply, by noticing the silence between two thoughts.

Common Obstacles and Gentle Reminders

When the path turns inward, the mind often brings old habits with it. It wants to achieve silence, prove progress, reach a finish line. But awareness cannot be achieved. It is already here. What clouds it are impatience and comparison.

Sometimes reflection turns into analysis. We start examining every thought as if we can outthink the mind. But true seeing is softer. It is like sitting beside a flowing river, watching without judging, without trying to stop the water. Understanding comes naturally when there is no struggle to understand.

At other times subtle pride appears: I am becoming special. It hides behind good intentions. The moment we claim ownership of clarity, fog returns. Awareness is humble by nature. It does not announce itself. It simply shines.

There are also days when stillness feels distant, when restlessness or sadness fills the heart. That too is part of rhythm. We do not fail when peace wavers. We learn that stillness does not depend on mood or circumstance. It is the steady pulse beneath change.

Gentleness is the key. Each time attention drifts, it can return. Not through strain, but through remembering. We are not fixing the mind. We are remembering the space in which the mind appears. That remembrance itself is a kind of grace.

How This Connects to What Came Before

Everything we explored so far quietly leads here. Each idea and story was a rope across the river, helping us see this: what we seek has never been outside us.

We learned that restlessness is not the enemy. It is energy waiting for direction. We studied the mind and saw its brilliance and its traps. We learned how the gunas color mood and perception. We saw how karma shapes experience and how awareness loosens the loop. We learned to bring practice into daily rhythm through breath, devotion, and stillness.

All these threads now meet in one movement. We move from what changes to the one who notices change.

Inquiry does not reject the world. It lets the world rest in perspective. Every part of life, family, work, joy, pain, becomes a mirror reminding us of what we truly are.

Then the earlier practices stop feeling like separate steps. They become natural expressions of understanding. Stillness flows into motion. Awareness breathes through action. Love becomes presence. Self inquiry is not apart from what came before. It is the flowering of it.

A Quiet Pause

There are moments when we realize we have been holding life too tightly.
Thought has been speaking nonstop, and we have been listening as if it is the only voice.

Then a small gap appears.
A pause between two thoughts.
A quiet behind the noise.

We do not have to fill it.
We do not have to name it.
We only have to notice it.

For a few breaths, rest there.
Let the world continue.
Let the mind move if it wants to.

And feel what remains when we stop chasing.
A simple awareness. Present. Clear. Unmoved.

Reflection for the Reader

Pause for a quiet moment. Let the world continue its hum in the background. Notice how awareness is already here, not something to summon, but something that never left. Every sound, every breath, every sensation appears within it.

Now ask softly.

Who is aware of this moment?

Where does a thought come from before it arrives?

And when it passes, what remains?

Do not rush to answer. Let the question rest. Sometimes silence replies more clearly than words. In that silence notice there is no struggle to be anyone and no effort to hold anything.

There is only the gentle sense of being, simple, steady, peaceful. That is not something we create through practice. It is what we have always been beneath seeking.

Closing

When awareness deepens, life does not become distant. It becomes more intimate. The same world remains, but we begin to see from stillness rather than struggle.

If you are a mother, listening deepens, not only to words, but to what the heart of your child is trying to say. If you are a father, guidance becomes steadier, less reactive, more supportive. If you are a partner, love becomes less possessive and more spacious, a place where both can breathe. If you are a worker or student, attention ripens into care and each task becomes less about outcome and more about offering.

Joy and sorrow still visit. Success and loss still come and go. Yet something beneath remains untouched. The one who observes knows this too will pass. And in that knowing, life becomes lighter.

Living as the witness does not mean retreating from the world. It means walking through it with open eyes, seeing all, holding less, letting life move in its rhythm. Outer actions continue, but the inner weight begins to fall away. We live not as the storm, but as the sky that holds it.

This is the quiet freedom the sages pointed to, awareness living as itself. And as this recognition stabilizes, a final question naturally rises. How do we carry this seeing into every act, every relationship, every ordinary moment, so it becomes living truth.

That is where our journey turns next.

CHAPTER 12
LIVING THE ANSWER
AWARENESS IN MOTION

The Beginning of Living

There comes a quiet moment on the path when the search itself begins to soften. Not because every question has been answered, but because the need to keep searching loosens. The mind that once chased clarity begins to sense that what it longed for was never really elsewhere.

Life still moves. Work, family, love, disappointment, effort, rest. The days still bring their changes. Yet beneath them, a quieter current begins to be felt. Not excitement. Not achievement. A simple ease.

This is the beginning of living differently. Not dramatically. Not as a sudden transformation others would easily notice. It is a shift so gentle that only the heart may recognize it at first. Instead of asking, What must I do to become free, something quieter begins to appear: What I sought has always been nearer than I thought.

The seeker who once strained toward light begins to live with a little more lightness. The urge to prove, fix, and grasp begins to weaken. Ordinary things start to feel sufficient again. A morning sky. A shared meal. A few minutes of silence. Nothing outward has become extraordinary, yet life begins to feel less divided.

True understanding does not always end in revelation. Often it ripens into ordinary grace. We still answer messages, lose patience, recover, and continue. But somewhere within, there is more room. Life no longer feels only like something happening to us. It begins to feel like something moving through us.

This is not escape from life. It is intimacy with life. Not withdrawal into silence, but a quieter way of being present while life unfolds.

When the Framework Becomes Lived

From the beginning, this book has been tracing a simple movement. We began with fog, the confusion that makes life feel heavy even when everything appears outwardly intact. We looked at the mind and saw that it is both the place where confusion gathers and the place where clarity can return. We saw how the gunas color the inner weather, how karma shapes the movement of life, how prana carries energy and attention, and how devotion, stillness, and inquiry each open a different doorway into the same truth.

When these are understood only as ideas, they remain separate. But when they begin to ripen in life, they form a single living framework.

We begin to recognize fog more quickly when it forms. We begin to sense whether the mind is clear, restless, or heavy. We begin to notice that actions leave an inner residue, and that awareness can soften the chain before it hardens. We begin to feel when breath is scattered and when it is steady. We begin to understand that love can soften what force cannot, and that stillness is not far away but quietly waiting beneath thought.

Then the framework stops feeling like a structure outside us. It begins to feel like a language for what is already happening within us. Life becomes more intelligible. Not easier in every outer way, but less confusing inwardly.

This is where understanding begins to turn into living.

Awareness in Motion

Awareness is not something we visit. It is what has been here all along. When the mind grows quiet enough to notice, even simple moments begin to feel different. Walking, speaking, listening, waiting. Each is carried by a silent presence that does not need effort in order to be.

To live in awareness is not to sit apart from the world. It is to move within it without becoming lost so easily. The body moves. The mind thinks. Words are spoken. Feelings rise and fall. Yet something remains open and still, like space around every sound.

This changes the texture of daily life. We walk and feel the contact of our feet with the ground. We listen and notice not only words, but tone, silence, and presence. We speak with a little more care because we no longer need every sentence to defend the self.

The world is not a distraction from clarity. It is where clarity becomes real. Laundry, cooking, driving, answering a message, sitting quietly before sleep. None of these are outside the path. They are the place where the path becomes lived.

Awareness in motion does not ask us to be perfect. It asks only for return. Even forgetting becomes part of the movement, because the moment we notice we have drifted is already the moment of return. Awareness was not lost. Attention had simply wandered.

What changes is not only what we do, but how we dwell in it. Work becomes less strained. Rest becomes less guilty. Relationships become less entangled in demand. Breath becomes something we feel again, not merely something that happens in the background.

When awareness enters action, life stops feeling only like a list of things to manage. It begins to feel more rhythmic, more spacious, more sincere. Not because difficulty vanishes, but because inner resistance begins to soften.

The Mind, the Heart, and the Weight of Action

Much of our exhaustion does not come from action itself. It comes from the fog around action. The mind fills work with comparison, fear, pressure, and self-measurement. The heart tightens around outcome. The sense of I claims every success and every failure. Then even simple effort becomes heavy.

But when the earlier understanding begins to mature, something shifts. We remember that the mind is an instrument, not the whole of what we are. We notice when rajas is pushing too hard, when tamas is thickening into avoidance, when sattva is quietly present. We see how old impressions are trying to turn this moment into a repetition of the past. We feel how breath changes before the mind admits its tension. And because we see more clearly, we do not get pulled so quickly into the same old loops.

Action remains, but weight begins to leave it. A tree offers fruit without asking to be praised. The sun gives light without keeping score. In the same way, we can begin to do what is needed without making each result a verdict on who we are.

This does not make action passive. It makes it cleaner. We

care, but with less tightening. We act sincerely, but with less inner strain. Mistakes still happen, but they do not wound the same way. Success may still come, but it does not need to inflate the self in the same way.

When the sense of ownership loosens, effort becomes lighter. The same work may remain, but the heaviness begins to leave it. We act, and then we allow life to move as it will. Something in us stops clenching around the outcome. This is not indifference. It is participation without unnecessary weight.

Relationship as the Place of Ripening

One of the clearest places this change appears is in relationship. It is easy to feel clear in solitude. Relationship reveals where we still cling, defend, fear, expect, or demand.

But relationship can also become one of the quiet places where wisdom ripens. When awareness matures, other people stop being only obstacles, mirrors for approval, or roles in our inner drama. They begin to appear more fully as lives in their own right, carrying their own burdens, longings, and confusions.

This softens something. Listening deepens. Defensiveness weakens a little. We begin to notice when the past is trying to speak through the present. We begin to feel the difference between reacting from an old wound and responding from clarity.

Even conflict changes its flavor. It still hurts. It still tests us. But it no longer has to become a full war of identity. Space enters. A pause. A breath. A willingness to see more than one side.

Love becomes less possessive and more spacious. Care becomes less anxious and more steady. Forgiveness becomes possible not because everything has become easy, but because we no longer want to keep carrying the same inner burden.

This is where devotion matures in daily life. Not as sentiment, but as tenderness strong enough to remain open.

Signs That Clarity Is Becoming Natural

The clearest signs of inner change are often small. We recover more quickly after being disturbed. We speak more softly where we once would have struck. We stop replaying one moment for hours. We forgive without making a ceremony of it. We notice beauty without needing to own it. We feel gratitude without having to manufacture it. These are not grand achievements. They are signs that the inner knots are loosening.

A person growing in freedom still feels sorrow, frustration, uncertainty, and tenderness. But these experiences no longer define the whole of life so completely. The mind still moves, yet something beneath it remains less shaken.

There is often more simplicity too. Less appetite for needless conflict. Less fascination with proving. Less hunger to be constantly seen. More capacity to remain quiet, to remain human, to remain present.

This freedom is not cold detachment. It is warmth without entanglement. Participation without drowning. A life that still feels deeply, but does not become so easily imprisoned by every passing inner weather.

The sages used the phrase jivanmukti, freedom while living, for this. Not a distant achievement, but a gradual inner release. The body lives. The mind moves. The world continues. Yet something essential is no longer bound in the same way.

The Ordinary Made Luminous

In the end, wisdom does not take us away from ordinary life. It returns us to it more fully. We come back to the same kitchen, the same street, the same family, the same unfinished tasks, the same changing world. But what has shifted is the way we meet them. There is a little less hardness. A little less fear. A little more room for breath, patience, and sincerity.

If you are a mother, nurturing becomes calmer and less draining. Love flows with less resistance. If you are a father, guidance becomes steadier and more present. If you are a partner, love becomes freer and listening grows deeper. If you are a worker, an artist, a leader, or a student, effort becomes lighter as purpose replaces pressure. If you are a spiritual seeker, the path begins to feel less like striving and more like remembering.

And even if you are simply living an ordinary day, something may begin to feel less ordinary about it. Not because the day changed, but because awareness entered it more fully.

The same mind still thinks. The same hands still move. Joy and sorrow still visit. Yet the foundation grows quieter. Life begins to feel less like struggle against circumstance and more like participation in a larger harmony.

When the heart abides in this steadiness, every breath becomes remembrance, every act becomes offering, and every moment becomes enough.

A Quiet Pause

There is a moment when effort softens.
Not because life has become simple,
but because we have stopped demanding
that it be different.
A breath arrives and leaves.
A thought passes.
A small sound fades into silence.
And something steady remains.
Not far away.
Not hidden.
Only quiet.
Rest there for a moment.
Let the day be exactly what it is.
Let nothing be added.
Let nothing be removed.
This is not a special state.
It is the beginning of living.

Reflection for the Reader

Pause for a moment. Let awareness rest, not on any object, but in itself. Notice the breath moving, thoughts rising and fading, sounds passing through.

Ask quietly:

Who is aware of this breath?
Who notices this thought come and go?
When everything changes, what remains?

Let the questions rest without hurry. No answer needs to be forced.

Then turn gently toward the life already in front of us. A meal, a conversation, a small task, a moment of waiting.

What happens when even one ordinary moment is met with full attention, without inner argument, without hurry, without resistance?

Perhaps this is where living begins to change. Not in some distant event, but here, where awareness enters the simplest act and makes it whole.

Closing

When understanding ripens, it does not remove us from life. It brings us more fully into it. We return to the same world, but something inside has shifted. We no longer move only as seekers. We begin to live from a stillness we can carry. And its proof appears not in grand moments, but in small ones.

A breath before we answer.
A softer tone where an old reaction used to rise.
A patience we did not have before.
A forgiveness that finally becomes possible.

Life still moves, but we are not pulled as hard.
This is the quiet promise at the heart of the journey. Not that life becomes perfect, but that it becomes transparent. Not that difficulty disappears, but that we are less divided within it. Not that we become something new, but that we begin to rest more naturally in what has always been here.

And so the journey returns to where it began. Not upward, but inward. Not toward something newly acquired, but toward the simple recognition of what we have never truly been apart from.

EPILOGUE – THE QUIET RETURN

The Quiet Return

There comes a moment when words no longer point forward. They turn softly back toward ourselves. What felt distant begins to feel familiar. What felt hidden begins to breathe quietly in everything.

This is not the end of the journey. It is a return to simplicity, to presence, to the wonder that has always been near.

We began with fog, with confusion and noise. We looked at the play of the mind, the colors of the gunas, and the quiet law that shapes cause and effect. Through all of it, one truth kept whispering. What we seek is not elsewhere. It is the one who seeks.

As the mind begins to rest, life itself becomes the teacher. A small act of kindness carries the same meaning as meditation. A single breath feels like prayer. Stillness does not belong to distant places. It unfolds in the midst of living.

The wise have spoken in different tongues, but their silence says the same thing. Truth is not owned by any path or belief. It is revealed wherever the heart is sincere.

A lily opens because it cannot help but open. The sun rises not to impress, but because light must shine. In the same way, awareness flowers in its own time, quietly, without striving. To behold such simple grace is to glimpse a sacred order behind all things.

We begin to sense that life moves with an intelligence greater than our plans. In that seeing, the urge to control softens, and gratitude takes its place. Ordinary things become luminous again, the sound of wind through trees, the warmth of tea in our hands, the pause between two breaths.

Each is a doorway back to the same stillness we once searched for. And then a prayer rises, not from memory, but from the quiet ground of being itself.

The Prayer of Wholeness

Sarve bhavantu sukhinah
Sarve santu niramayah
Sarve bhadrani pashyantu
Ma kashchid duhkha bhag bhavet

Translation:

May all beings be happy.
May all be free from illness.
May all see what is auspicious.
May no one suffer any sorrow.

When we say, "May all be happy," something deep within us

remembers. The joy we wish for others is not separate from our own. That prayer itself is the heart awakening.

We do not have to change the world to make it sacred. We only have to see it clearly, alive, connected, and already whole.

And so we return to our homes, our families, our work, our quiet mornings, carrying not new knowledge, but a lighter gaze. The world is the same, yet it glows now from within.

LIVING THE FRAMEWORK

A framework matters only when it becomes lived. What we have explored in these pages is not meant to remain as thought alone, but to become a quieter way of seeing.

When we begin to notice the movements of mind, energy, and awareness in ordinary life, something changes. Work becomes less mechanical. Relationships become more revealing. Stillness becomes easier to recognize in the middle of movement.

Then the framework is no longer something we study. It becomes something we live.

And perhaps that is enough. Not to become someone new, but to live with a little more clarity, a little more steadiness, and a little more remembrance of what has always been here.

NOTE FROM NANDI

This book is not teaching. It is a remembering. Each chapter, each metaphor, each quiet pause was written as a mirror, not to show something new, but to help us recognize what was always here.

The words came through a journey of questioning, of falling and rising again, and of learning that silence can say more than philosophy ever can. If any part of this work has touched you, it is not because of its author, but because truth already lives in us, quietly, patiently, waiting to be noticed.

This is not an ending. It is a beginning.

Close the book, and keep walking, gently, attentively. Every breath, every sound, every person we meet can become a verse in the same living scripture.

If you would like to continue exploring these reflections, visit **closertotheself.com**, where these ideas will continue to unfold over time in a simple and practical way.

May your journey be light, your heart steady, and your seeing clear. May peace follow you like a shadow that never leaves.

Om Shanti.

GLOSSARY

Core Concepts

The Self (True Self): The changeless, serene, untouched, and whole essence of existence. Its recognition is presented as the highest goal, from which health, joy, efficiency, and clarity flow naturally. It is the quiet presence, the witnessing awareness behind all movement and change, often glimpsed in the stillness between thoughts.

Ignorance (The Fog): The condition that blurs perception. It is the forgetting of our true Self. It covers the light but never destroys it.

Jivanmukti: Freedom while living. It is marked by ease, simplicity, steadiness, and quiet compassion.

Moksha (Liberation): The end of inner compulsion. It is the recognition of what was never truly trapped, when the momentum of rebirth no longer needs to continue.

The Structure of Reality

Brahman: The changeless field of pure existence, consciousness, and fullness (sat chit ananda). It is the foundation upon which everything else rises and falls, remaining undivided even as it appears as many.

Maya (The Creative Veil): The lens through which the single reality appears as a diverse world. It is not falsehood, but the creative power that projects the movie of life onto the screen of awareness.

Ishvara (The Cosmic Mind): The expression of Brahman when Maya is dominated by sattva (clarity). It is the total intelligence and order that holds creation in balance.

Jiva (Jivas): Individual experiencers. The countless points of experience through which consciousness moves through struggle and learning.

Samsara (The Turning Wheel): The continuing cycle of birth, experience, and rebirth, driven by unfinished momentum in the mind. It continues until understanding loosens the push behind it.

The Functions of the Mind

Antahkarana (Inner Instrument): The inner system through which experience is received, interpreted, and stored. The mind is described as an orchestra of subtle instruments which, when out of rhythm, create inner turbulence.

Manas (The Messenger): The gatherer of sensory impressions. It connects the senses to the inner world, reporting what is perceived.

Buddhi (The Light of Discernment): The guiding intelligence. It evaluates, discriminates, and shines clearly, asking: "Is this true? Is this useful? Is this kind?"

Ahamkara (The Claimant, Ego): The sense of "I" that gives individuality. It claims ownership of actions, thoughts, and feelings, turning experience into personal pride or personal wound.

Chitta (The Storehouse): Memory, and the repository for impressions (samskara) and tendencies (vasana). It is the soil of destiny where thoughts plant seeds.

The Qualities of Nature

Gunas: Three qualities that weave everything in creation and determine how we feel, act, and perceive the world.

Sattva: Clarity, light, purity, harmony, joy, and wisdom. Cultivating sattva supports inner peace.

Rajas: Motion, activity, desire, ambition, and restlessness. It fuels effort and creation, but when unbalanced it leads to fatigue and agitation.

Tamas: Inertia, heaviness, confusion, dullness, and resistance. When prolonged, it becomes stagnation and denial.

Karma and the Cycle of Action

Karma: Action, and the law of cause and effect. Every thought, word, and deed plants a seed, shaping experience and restoring balance. It operates as a subtle intelligence, not as punishment.

Sanchita Karma: The total store of dormant, accumulated impressions.

Prarabdha Karma: The portion of sanchita karma that has ripened and is unfolding as the circumstances of the present life.

Agami Karma: The fresh seeds planted through present actions and intentions, shaping what comes next.

Phala (Fruit of Action): The result of karma that ripens when cause, condition, and opportunity align.

Samskara (Impression): A faint, subtle seed or trace left upon the mind by every action, desire, or thought.

Vasana (Tendency): A strong inclination that forms when repeated samskaras gather strength. It becomes a subtle pull toward certain actions, reactions, and choices.

Vritti (Thought Wave): A ripple on the surface of the mind. A thought that surfaces when a vasana is stirred.

Kama (Desire): A thought we identify with that becomes "I want." It focuses the mind and pulls energy in a particular direction.

Trishna (Craving): Desire that hardens into restlessness and attachment, eventually compelling action.

The Path of Yoga

Yoga: Harmonized disciplines that support the recognition of the Self. Integral Yoga is the blending of these paths, head, heart, hands, and inner stillness, into one daily rhythm.

Jnana Yoga (Path of Understanding): The path of wisdom and self inquiry (atma vichara). It uses reflection and discernment to remove confusion and see clearly.

Bhakti Yoga (Path of Love): The path of devotion that purifies emotion and softens separation. It turns daily acts into offerings of love and gratitude.

Karma Yoga (Path of Action): The path of doing without attachment to results. Action performed as service or contribution, which loosens the grip of ego.

Raja Yoga (Path of Stillness): The path of inner mastery, discipline, meditation, and pranayama. It calms the waves of thought so awareness can shine.

Prana and Breath

Prana (Life Current): The vital current that links body, breath, and mind. Breath is the doorway. Prana is the current behind it. When prana is scattered, the mind scatters. When prana steadies, a pause appears.

Pancha Pranas (Five Movements of Prana):

- **Prana Vayu:** Inward and upward current, linked with breath and the heart area
- **Apana Vayu:** Downward grounding current, linked with release and elimination
- **Samana Vayu:** Balancing current, linked with digestion and settling energy
- **Udana Vayu:** Rising current, linked with speech, expression, and lift
- **Vyana Vayu:** Circulating current, spreading through the whole system

Pranayama (Working with Breath and Energy): Using breath to steady prana. Less about forcing breath and more about restoring rhythm, so attention becomes calmer and clearer.

Practices and Inner Skills

Prajna (Clear Seeing with Warmth): Clear seeing that includes compassion. The head and heart move together.

Viveka (Discernment): The ability to tell the difference between what changes and what remains.

Atma Vichara (Self Inquiry): Turning attention inward and asking "Who am I," not to collect an answer, but to trace the sense of "I" back to awareness.

Abhyasa (Steady Practice): Returning again and again to the chosen focus without harshness.

Vairagya (Non Clinging): The quiet loosening that happens when we stop gripping thoughts, outcomes, and identities.

Dhyana (Meditation): The flow of attention resting steadily, without being pulled again and again.

Shanta Atma (Peaceful Self): The peaceful Self that does not have to be earned, only remembered.

ACKNOWLEDGMENTS

These pages come from a long stream of understanding carried by the sages, and kept alive by teachers and seekers across time.

I am grateful for the Gita, the Ramayana, and the Upanishads, and for the quiet help they offer when life feels unclear.

Above all, I bow to my Guru, who showed me the real meaning behind these pointers and helped me live them in ordinary days.

Thank you, the reader, for your sincerity and your patience as we walk this together.

APPENDIX A

Chapter Overview and Reflections

An expanded guide to accompany your journey through **Closer to the Self**

Part I: The Human Condition

1. The Fog of Confusion

- **The Fog**: Life is present but blurred by ignorance.
- **Not All Fog Is Everywhere**: Strengths remain; clarity already shines in parts of us.
- **The Short-Circuiting of Energies**: Noble qualities can distort into their opposites.
- **The Third Eye and Horizontal Vision**: Past and future pull us away from the present; the witnessing Self.
- **The Dusty Mirror**: The mind covered by restlessness and desire.
- **The Search Outside**: Outward-flowing attention and the turn inward.
- **What the Sages Point To**: Fog covers but never destroys; the rope and snake parable.

• **The Modern Restlessness**: Noise, screens, and the storm of distraction.

• **Hope Beyond the Fog**: Ignorance is a condition, not our essence.

• **Reflection for the Reader**: Naming our own fog.

• **Closing**: Life becomes more meaningful; fullness within everyday roles.

2. The Mirror Within

• **The Mirror and the Orchestra**: The mind as a mirror; the inner instruments that create harmony or noise.

• **The Flow of a Moment**: How experience moves through perception, reaction, and memory, forming fog or clarity.

• **The Four Functions of the Mind**: Manas, Buddhi, Ahamkara, and Chitta shaping every response.

• **Manas**: The messenger of sensory impressions.

• **Buddhi**: The light of discernment.

• **Ahamkara**: The claimant shaping the sense of I.

• **Chitta**: The storehouse of impressions and tendencies.

• **How the Fog Forms Inside**: When the inner instruments lose harmony.

• **The Role of Prana**: The vital current beneath the mind linking body, breath, and awareness.

• **The Fog Begins to Clear**: Sunlight through clouds; a still lake reflecting the sky.

• **Reflection for the Reader**: Observing the inner orchestra in action.

• **Closing**: Tending the lamp of clarity through meditation, reflection, and devotion.

3. Threads of the Self

• **The Threads of Nature**: Experience woven from Sattva, Rajas, and Tamas.

• **The Three Qualities**: Light, motion, and inertia.

• **The Meaning of Karma**: Action, intention, and the seeds of destiny.

• **The Three Types of Karma**: Sanchita, Prarabdha, and Agami.

• **The Cycle of Inner Seeds**: From impression to craving to action and return.

• **Freedom Within Karma**: The art of acting without bondage.

• **Reflection for the Reader**: Tracing emotion to its seed.

• **Closing**: The light beyond cause and effect; living fully yet inwardly free.

6. The Flow Within

• **The Breath of Life**: Prana as the silent current linking seen and unseen.

• **The Hidden Current**: Energy as quiet vitality, not agitation.

• **Breath as Mirror**: Breath reflecting the mind.

• **The Four Movements of Breath**: Inhalation, retention, exhalation, stillness.

• **How This Connects to What Came Before**: Prana uniting mind, gunas, and karma.

• **Reflection for the Reader**: Watching breath and sensing the still awareness behind motion.

• **Closing: The Quiet Rhythm of Existence**: Balance revealed when resistance ends.

7. The Turning Wheel

• **The Continuity of Consciousness**: Karma extending through lifetimes.

• **The Law Behind Rebirth**: Cause seeking fulfillment through time.

• **Between Two Lives**: Rest, review, and renewal.

• **Breaking the Cycle**: Freedom through understanding.

• **The Thread of Memory**: Glimpses of continuity.

• **Reflection for the Reader**: Observing repeating patterns and the still witness.

• **Closing: Freedom Beyond Birth and Death**: Living from the unmoving center while the wheel turns.

Part III: The Path of Clarity

8. The Way of Yoga

• **The Four Paths**: Action, devotion, meditation, and understanding.

• **The Purpose of Yoga**: Uniting all movements of life toward awareness.

• **Action as Offering**: Karma Yoga; work as worship, action without claim.

• **The Fire of Love**: Bhakti Yoga; devotion transforming emotion into surrender.

• **The Discipline of Mind**: Raja Yoga; concentration and stillness as gateways to peace.

• **The Inquiry of Truth**: Jnana Yoga; understanding as direct seeing.

• **Integration of Paths**: Harmony of head, heart, hands, and spirit.

• **Reflection for the Reader**: Noticing which path feels natural today.

• **Closing: One Path Within Many**: Every movement of life leading back to awareness.

9. The Fire of Devotion

• **The Call of the Heart**: The need for devotion in a restless age.

• **The Nature of Bhakti**: Love dissolving separation.

• **The Faces of Devotion**: Surrender, reverence, friendship, and service.

• **Mantra and Remembrance**: Sound and attention shaping awareness.

• **Reflection for the Reader**: Opening the heart in ordinary moments.

• **Closing**: When love matures into stillness, and stillness flowers into love.

10. The Silent Witness

• **The Nature of Meditation**: Resting the mind in its source.

• **The Stages of Practice**: Attention, observation, absorption.

• **The Witness Within**: Recognizing the observer behind experience.

• **Reflection for the Reader**: Sitting quietly and letting stillness speak.

• **Closing**: Living from stillness, not toward it.

11. The Question That Frees

• **The Mirror of Awareness**: Seeing clearly through self inquiry.

• **The Nature of Inquiry**: Who am I as living contemplation.

• **The Silence Behind Thought**: Awareness as constant background.

• **Reflection for the Reader**: Pausing to notice awareness as witness.

• **Closing**: Living as the witness; calm awareness transforming action.

12. The Living Light

• **The End of Seeking**: Insight as participation, not withdrawal.

• **Awareness in Motion**: Life itself as meditation.

• **Action Without Weight**: Acting fully, free from grasping.

• **Relationships as Reflection**: Meeting all as Self.

• **Integrating the Four Yogas**: Balance of understanding, devotion, stillness, and action.

• **Reflection for the Reader**: Seeing clarity shine through every breath and choice.

www.ingramcontent.com/pod-product-compliance
Lightning Source LLC
LaVergne TN
LVHW090516110826
845146LV00003B/876

* 9 7 9 8 9 9 5 7 8 6 1 0 8 *